P9-DWE-581

FAITHFUL
RESISTANCE

GOSPEL VISIONS FOR THE CHURCH
IN A TIME OF EMPIRE

RICK UFFORD-CHASE

"I believe that I shall see the goodness of God in the land of the living. Wait for God; be strong, and let your heart take courage; wait for God!"

Psalm 27:13-14

For Kitty - who makes time for me to write and to run rivers and who shapes me and steadies me in the work we share.

Table of Contents

Foreword

The voice of Jesus echoes off the mountain, carries on the wind, filling the air with sound and hope,

> *"Blessed are the poor…*
> *Blessed are the hungry…*
> *Blessed are those who weep…."*

The list continues and expands until the hated, excluded, defamed are blessed. By some miracle, this sermon reverberates to us, thousands of years and a world away from that particular mount. As followers of Christ, we not only read the words, we also try to understand and embody the syllables. Yet, because we are so removed from that time and place, many things elude our grasp.

Jesus ministered under the looming shadow of the Roman Empire, one of the most powerful forces in antiquity, known for its economic, cultural, political, and military influence. The Roman rulers were so tactical about their threats and intimidation that they dotted the sides of the roads with crucified bodies as a warning to the seditious. And even with those horrifying advisories, the disciples resisted. In this time when the Empire exalted the rich, full pleasure-seekers, Jesus reminds the crowd who is really blessed – the poor, hungry, and weeping.

Yet this sermon can present a problem for many of us, if we're not the sort of people who huddled among the rocks and ledges, trying to get as close to the feet of Jesus when he spoke. What happens when our churches have more in common with the Empire than the disciples? What if we find ourselves wrapped up in religious communities that serve the Empire in ways that we cannot even recognize? How can we resist the

Empire's impulses and influence when we are so much a part of them?

This is the crucial question for the church in our moment. As pastors, seminaries and church leaders worry about declining membership and budgets, we can easily be seduced by the idea that more money, power and consumption will save us. We imagine that serving a successful church means raising endowments, leveraging influence, and building institutions. Performance replaces worship. Marketing strategies take over evangelism efforts. Networking stands in for solidarity. We don't even know that we have been swept up into Empire-think, until we let those those words from the Sermon on the Mount jar us, reminding us that Jesus lifts up the poor, the hungry, and the weeping. In his words and deeds, Jesus reminds us how those who resist the lure of Empire are blessed.

When we begin to ask ourselves how we have been consumed by the allure of Empire we can lean into Rick Ufford-Chase's wise words. Rick Ufford-Chase, who has spent decades working with the poor, hungry, and weeping, has gathered a group of practitioners and thinkers who identify the ways in which we participate in Empire and remind us of our important task of resisting it. Voices from Mexican border towns, Black Lives Matter movements, Muslim neighbors and LGBTQ communities rise up to remind us how the church sometimes loses itself in the heart of the Empire.

But the story doesn't stop there. Books can easily dismantle decades of thought, but these authors take care to also construct a clear vision of what our churches, seminaries and denominations can look like while they resist Empire, giving us a glimpse of solidarity, subversion, and liberation.

The vast knowledge and experience in this volume is a gift to the church. It challenges my thinking, not only on an academic or philosophical level, but in my nuts and bolts ministry.

Through these words, I'm beginning to understand that ancient sermon. I'm learning how to embody the syllables, because I have these travelers surrounding me, offering me a model of faithful resistance.

Carol Howard Merritt

Introduction

The numbers are clear. The traditional Protestant churches in the United States like the one in which I was raised are in trouble. The Catholic Church is facing similar challenges, and it is increasingly clear that nondenominational, evangelical churches – particularly the megachurch versions – are impacted by many of the same realities that are squeezing those in my own Presbyterian tradition. By and large, we have become handmaidens to the Empire, a conundrum also confronted by Jesus, a Jew in first century Palestine, but made far more complicated by the remarkable level of complicity we all share in the project of Empire in our world today.

The Presbyterian Church (USA) has less than half the membership that our predecessor denominations had when my father took his first call at First Presbyterian Church in York, Pennsylvania in 1968, the last year Presbyterians experienced numerical growth as a national church. In spite of our best intentions, and the faithful witness of African American, Latino, Korean and many new immigrant churches, the reality of the Presbyterian Church in the United States is shared by most of our sister, Protestant denominations. We are overwhelmingly white, both culturally and demographically. We are aging fast, and the next generation shows little interest in rescuing our institution for its own sake. Many of those who once could be found in our pews on Sunday morning have opted out.

We have built an elegant corporate church structure for the church of yesterday that no longer effectively serves the church of today, and actually impedes our ability to create the church of tomorrow. Our functions of providing a sense of shared identity and connecting us for a common mission seem almost trivial in the face of a world now dominated by the internet, social media, and the ability to connect with others with shared interests around the world at the push of a button or the upload of a photo or video.

We are culture-bound: unable to see the ways in which we have twisted the meaning of our sacred text to justify our complicity in the Empire project. We are so caught up in all that it takes to survive in a globalized world, and so desperate in our search for meaning, that we miss the answers that are right in front of us in the sacred stories of God's people who have struggled with similar questions across millennia.

Too often, and in too many ways, we remain timid when we should be bold, fearful when we are called to be unafraid, and beholden to the principalities and powers when both the prophets of scripture and the prophets of today exhort us to rethink our allegiances. We have become the church of the Empire, the very thing Jesus urged both Jews and Gentiles of his own time to rise up against. We go through great theological contortions to prod the gospel into a justification for our comfort and complacency, and fail to recognize the vast spiritual pit that we dig for ourselves in the process.

I grew up in what was, in my opinion, about the best possible experience of mainline Christianity's glory days in the United States. I was four years old when my parents moved to York, Pennsylvania, and my dad joined the pastoral staff at First Presbyterian Church. In my earliest memories, I stand next to him, shaking hands with more than four hundred parishioners as they file out from each of two services on Sunday mornings. Cub Scouts and Vacation Bible School filled my summers at the church. We organized work projects to help people in the county after Hurricane Agnes hit. I accompanied my dad to countless visits with "shut-ins" – the elderly members of the church who could no longer get out and about. Junior High meant activities at the church twice a week. In high school, most of my social life revolved around youth group retreats, and I dated almost exclusively within that close-knit group of friends. Each Sunday morning at six, I had a job preparing the sanctuary, setting up the classrooms, and shoveling the snow to ready the church. I spent Saturdays acting as a coordinator and custodian for the many weddings that took place at the church each week. As a junior in high school, I committed to a year of intensive study to become a disciple of Jesus, preparing myself for a lifetime of service and leadership in the church. This was my world.

I see, in hindsight, that First Presbyterian, like so many others of our "mainline" churches across the country, prided itself on being theologically moderate. Some of our pastors leaned evangelical, while others were more traditional: trained to be theologically curious and emotionally reserved. The preaching was articulate and intelligent. Though these were turbulent times – the Civil Rights Movement, the "race riots[1]," the Vietnam War, and women's liberation – my memory is that the sanctum of First Presbyterian Church remained relatively unaffected and serene.

In 1965, First Presbyterian merged with a much smaller, African-American congregation called Faith Presbyterian, when the latter could no longer keep its doors open. Though this was a bold statement of unity in 1965, it didn't appear to translate to political engagement in the midst of the Civil Rights Movement, nor did it fundamentally change the culture of the church. Still, it shaped me in significant ways. If it hadn't been for the church, I really could have gone all the way through high school without stepping outside the intricate and tightly-choreographed dance that was deeply embedded into our society - a dance designed to keep me worlds apart from anyone who was different than me.

This Presbyterian church, fully comfortable in and with the dominant culture, looked just like thousands of other churches across the U.S. at the time. Some of them are holding on even in these very different times, four decades later. Good people fill

---

[1] The racial protest in the streets of York were eerily similar to the protests following Michael Brown's death in Ferguson in 2014.

these churches and, in many instances, they do good work in the community and around the world. At critical moments over the last four decades as the social safety net has been systematically disassembled by the federal government, these churches have often provided care for the poorest people in the community. But at the end of the day, by and large, the folks who fill our pews in these churches located at the center of our communities have been the winners in the social, political and economic structures that have defined our country for the last half-century. Even the word "mainline" that has come to be a common description of the traditional Protestant denominations in the United States itself refers to the privileged who live on the train lines that shuttle them back and forth between the inner cities and the suburbs.

I loved First Presbyterian Church, and I was grateful for the secure foundation, theological curiosity and strong grounding in my faith that it provided me. I love the elders in that community who shaped me, and value the friendships with my peers formed there. Still, it is the church of yesterday. Attempts today to recreate its model for ministry offer little or no promise for the church of tomorrow.

The 25th chapter of Matthew begins with the story of the ten bridesmaids. We are told that ten bridesmaids are waiting for the bridegroom through the night, unsure when he will come to take them into the party. Five of them trim their lamps, assuring that they will have oil to spare when the Bridegroom arrives, while the foolish ones pay no attention to their oil as the night, and their waiting, goes on. Sure enough, we're told, when the Bridegroom arrives the five who are prepared are taken into the festivities, while those who did not pay attention are left behind (Matthew 25:1-12).

The most compelling biblical scholarship on the 25th Chapter of Matthew suggests that this is a warning to us, a call to be aware, to be watching, because something big is about to happen at a time that we cannot pre-determine. It is a story for a moment like ours, in which we teeter on the knife-edge between the church we have been and the new thing that God calls us to be.

For good and ill, the Protestant Church in the United States has a history of more than three centuries in which we have defined the social mores of our society. We provided the theological justification for the theft of the land we now inhabit and on which every one of our churches sits. We presented the blueprints for our country's system of governance. Our members have been the captains of industry, presiding over the creation of phenomenal wealth – often on the backs of people who have been pushed to almost unimaginable (for those of us who benefit from the dominant paradigm) destitution and oppression. Even while a few of our leaders offered a prophetic voice calling us out of the slave economy, our churches offered the moral framework and rationale that provided the theological justification for the practice of slavery.

We embraced Manifest Destiny and went out to save the world with education, healthcare and "modernization" through our missionary movements. Too often that missionary zeal rode in on the coattails of western colonization and paved the way for the attendant, massive transfer of wealth from the global south to the global north. In the early 1900's, we articulated a social gospel to lift up those on the margins of our society, but we rarely questioned the fundamental principalities and powers that actively impoverished so many. By the middle of the last century, we had fully embraced the corporatization of the church, and found ourselves increasingly beholden to the government as its apologist.

A few courageous religious leaders did say "no" to segregation, often losing their pulpits in the process. Some campus pastors supported young men as they burned their draft cards during the Vietnam War. Over five hundred congregations defied the Reagan Administration and declared themselves "Sanctuaries" for Central American refugees in the 1980's. Our national church bodies have consistently called for economic justice and condemned the vagaries of unbridled capitalism, and our denominations have led a public witness through the use of corporate engagement and divestment from companies whose values run counter to our own.

Still, our commitment to social witness has too often happened in spite of the lack of support from local congregations rather than because of their encouragement. Most of our congregations appear to have forgotten that we are the church of Jesus, or we have so badly convoluted the meaning of Jesus' story as to make it meaningless. This should be no surprise, for it has happened repeatedly throughout our two-thousand-year history, just as it happened to the people of Israel who were our forebears for millennia before that.

Each time we forget, the Spirit moves and God breaks forth with a renewed vision of our calling as the followers of Jesus – the upstart activist against the Empire of his time and a threat to the religious and political authorities. Throughout our history, it has been the greatest of callings to sit with those expectant bridesmaids, to be alive, aware, and invited by God to help something new break forth.

This is such a moment. We have a chance to reclaim the fundamental values that have re-grounded our church in similar moments throughout our history. To do so, we will need to let go of the internal anxiety within our church that dominates so much of our discourse today. While we worry about our diminishing membership or panic about lost income for our budgets, the spirit is beginning to move. As we struggle to maintain choirs and Christian Education programs designed for a different time, we see glimpses that God is at work and that we are called to ask different questions. In the midst of stress-induced headaches over cutting church staffs, we see signs that our members are actually re-energized by the opportunity to practice the art of ministry to and with one another.

This book is for those who dream that another church is possible and know that God still works among us. It is for those of us who believe that Jesus makes an outrageous claim on our lives. We are bound together by our shared desire to be unflinchingly honest about the best and the worst we have been throughout our history, and our shared conviction that God calls us to a new thing.

This is not a book that offers a "how to" that will save the institution of the church. Rather, it is a "what if" book. What if we moved to the margins? What if we embraced our calling as followers of Jesus and opened ourselves to God's call across the ages to be a witness to life in the midst of death, possibility in a time of despair, and justice against all odds?

In my Presbyterian tradition, we pride ourselves that we are "reformed and always being reformed" by God, by which we mean that it is our obligation to understand the signs of the times and seek constantly to understand God's deepest desires for us as we try to live faithfully in our historical moment. I love that notion of what it means to be reformed, and think that is useful to all of us who are struggling to be faithful in the twenty-first century.

Inspired by that commitment to understand our current context, the first half of this book names five of the "signs of the times" that I believe present a huge challenge to the church of Jesus in the United States today:

- Is it possible to move - with Jesus - from the heart of Empire to the margins of Empire?

- What would it look like to admit our complicity in the systems of white supremacy that continue to distance us from one another, and from God?

- What if we were to re-imagine our relationship with creation in a way that would offer genuine hope for our children and grandchildren, and their children and grandchildren?

- Could we transform the reality that much of the violence in the world today is grounded in the exclusivist claims of our religious traditions?

- Is it possible to overcome our fear of difference and create communities that model genuine welcome and a place of belonging in a culture dominated by the conviction that difference is a threat?

Also, in the Presbyterian tradition that grounds me, we strive for decision making that involves all of us in discerning God's will for our communities. The second half of this book offers fodder for those who are discerning what it might look like to create new faith communities that have the capacity to respond to the challenges of our time:

- What might it look like to form local worshiping communities that have the strength to stand against Empire values that are antithetical to our core convictions as Christians?

- Given the significant challenges that confront us in this time, how might we rethink our understanding of pastoral leadership and the task of theological formation?

- What if we re-defined Christian Mission to be the task of accompaniment – standing with partners in our communities and around the world who have committed themselves to resist the inhumanity of Empire and practices of domination that impede Jesus' vision of what real community can look like?

- What if we connected with one another in new ways that break down our institutional structures which are barriers to creativity and forged new ways to build relationships of trust and daring?

- What if we intentionally deconstructed the massive bureaucracies of our national church structure and re-tooled to become the church of the future?

No one person can offer the experience or the breadth of diversity that will encompass who we are called to become or what we are called to do as followers of Jesus. For that reason, I have asked a dozen colleagues and mentors who have challenged my own thinking and practice as a Christian to help me take on each of these "what ifs."

Together we are gay, straight and transgender; white and people of color; older and younger; men and women; inside church structures and outside; Christian and Muslim. Though most of these contributors are Presbyterian because that is my world, all of us are working in contexts that pay little attention to traditional denominational identities. We believe that we can do better, that God is not finished with us yet, and that nothing could be more fulfilling or exciting than a full embrace of the unknown that God has in store for us. Just as importantly, we believe that God's people must stand against violence and injustice and hold ourselves and our institutions accountable for the things we do that do not honor God's vision for us as it is laid out in our sacred text.

Finally, a few words about my own background, which is full of contradictions that I am slow to recognize, but try to be quick to admit. Socially progressive evangelicals in the U.S., Pentecostals in poor churches in Latin America, and liberationist movements and theologies grounded in churches around the world shape and form me. I am not much interested in "conservative" vs. "liberal" labels that serve mostly to polarize us, and I have very little use for the rigidity of fundamentalists. Socially conservative Christians, who too often act as the handmaidens of economic and political forces of domination in the United States, weary me. Similarly, though I am politically liberal in what passes for political discourse in the United States today, I have little patience for unthinking liberalism or sloganeering, especially when espoused by people of faith. Though I am deeply critical of my country, I can't imagine choosing to leave it. I consider it a high calling to exhort each other to live up to the best of our civic ideals, second only to my higher calling to do the same for the church.

I try to be both passionate in my convictions, and humble in my awareness that my own experience is not the center of God's universe. I know that God isn't finished with me yet. I have intentionally chosen jobs that place me just far enough from the center of the institution of the Presbyterian Church (USA) to be able to speak uncomfortable truths and try new things that challenge the status quo, while still close enough to have some hope that I might influence our future. The church is my home, and I am unwilling to abandon it due to the unfaithfulness that appears to be its constant condition.

I am an organizer and activist, most at home when participating in social movements, even while I recognize (especially in my interactions with my teenaged kids) that I am also deeply traditionalist and maybe even a little bit too conservative in my unwillingness to challenge institutional structures. Sometimes I wish I were more courageous. I have always been a bridge builder, and I am an unapologetic follower of Jesus Christ - whom I know best as the Prince of Peace.

Finally, I am white with significant financial resources and bodily secure. I am male, heterosexual, married and a father of three. Western institutions educated me. I am temporarily able-bodied and in my fifties. I hold a U.S. passport. That hits pretty much every single category of privilege I can imagine. Awareness of my unearned privilege, and a sense of obligation to those who do not carry similar privilege, drives my commitment to stand with those on the margins. Too often, I am compromised by the privilege I carry, which makes the brief moments of courage I have managed all the more poignant and meaningful.

And I might be wrong.

-Rick Ufford-Chase

Part One

Church in the Heart of Empire

Chapter 1
Confronting Empire at the Border

Can Anything Good Come from Nazareth?
Alison Harrington

In the gospels there is this little, almost forgettable, conversation between Philip and his friend Nathanael. Philip tells Nathanael, "Hey, you know the Messiah we have been waiting for? Well, I just met him; his name is Jesus son of Joseph from Nazareth."

Incredulously, Nathanael says, "Can anything good come out of Nazareth?"

For those of us who know how the story unfolds, Nathanael's question makes us smile, for we know that what comes out of the surprising backwater peasant village Nazareth is nothing less than the hope of the ages.

For those of us who are looking for hope today, Nathanael's question should give us pause, because too often, like Nathanael, we are looking for good news in all the wrong places. The exchange between these two friends asks us to shift our gaze from Rome, or even Jerusalem – the strongholds of the Empire – to Nazareth and the places of hopelessness and disrepute that end up being the strongholds of love and hope.

I begin here because who amongst us in the past several years has not said, "Can anything good come out of Arizona?" But what we are coming to realize is that the place that has been called a laboratory of racist anti-migrant legislation and practices, is also the place where radical resistance lead by undocumented organizers is inspiring our communities to push back and to create communities of hospitality and a grassroots movement for migrant justice.

As people living in the land of Sheriff Joe Arpaio, SB1070, Operation Streamline, a militarized border, prowling patrol vehicles, private prison operated detention centers, and deportations that tear apart families and devastate our communities, we are well acquainted with fear. But in the midst of this empire of fear, we remember the words of scripture, "perfect love casts out fear." And for us, the only way to be church within this Empire is to enact love in ways that disrupt the machinery of the Empire. But we did not arrive at this place of disruptive love on our own. Rather, the powerful acts of resistance and organizing lead by Latino community members inspired and guided us. When community members began to literally put their bodies on the line by getting underneath border patrol vehicles or surrounding these vehicles with human chains thereby preventing, if only for an hour or two, the detention and inevitable deportation of moms and dads, we began to ask ourselves, "how can the body of Christ begin to get in the way of the deportation machine?" It wasn't long before we found our answer in the work of sanctuary.

To many, Southside is known as "the sanctuary church." In the 1980's, civil war ripped through Central America, creating a desperate migration of people to the U.S. They were met by the refusal of the United States government to follow its own refugee policies and were deported back to the death squads from which they were running. In response, churches like Southside opened their doors, declaring sanctuary and creating an underground railroad for refugees. The movement drew to a close around 1992, and although the Sanctuary Movement had a rebirth in 2006, it had been more than thirty years since the congregation originally declared themselves a safe place for Central American refugees. But sanctuary was in our DNA, and as the numbers of deportations reached record numbers, and as we witnessed too many families in our own community torn apart, we again began to whisper, 'sanctuary'.

It wasn't long before that whisper was said aloud for anyone with ears to hear on May 12, 2014 when local father, Daniel Neyoy Ruiz entered Sanctuary at Southside. When he left sanctuary after 28 days with a stay of deportation in his hand we were overjoyed that our prayers had been answered and we assumed that our work was done. Then we met Rosa.

Rosa Robles Loreto and her husband, Gerardo, began living in the U.S. in 1999. An accountant from Hermosillo, she knew that working as a housecleaner in the U.S. would provide a better quality of life than working as an accountant in Mexico. When she and Gerardo discovered they were pregnant, they returned to Mexico believing that it was the right thing to do. After the second child was born, they decided to return to the U.S. in 2006. Now back in the U.S. they settled into life, attending a local Catholic Church, working, and, perhaps most importantly, cheering at their boys' little league games. But as happy as their life was, there was always the fear of deportation hanging over them. In 2010, on her way to work, this nightmare became a reality when Rosa was pulled over for a minor traffic violation and the police officer called the border patrol. After 61 days in detention, her family paid her bond and she began to fight her deportation order. When Rosa showed up at the Keep Tucson Together legal clinic that meets at Southside, she had three options: leave her family behind and return to Mexico, try to evade deportation by moving to another address, or enter into sanctuary and fight for her right to be with her family. On August 7th, Rosa entered into sanctuary and began to fight.

With both Daniel and Rosa's case, we saw our sanctuary work moving along three trajectories. The first was our short term goal of providing Rosa and her family hospitality. We prepared a room for Rosa and set up a second room, which we affectionately called the "solidarity suite," for the dozens of volunteers who accompanied Rosa in rotating shifts. And then there were the prayer vigils; every night at 7pm we gathered to pray because we knew if we didn't ground ourselves in the daily practice of prayer we would lose heart.

The second trajectory was the campaign work itself as we mobilized the community to call for Rosa to be granted a stay of deportation. We collected letters of support, advocated for the City Council and the Board of Supervisors to pass resolutions in support of Rosa, and knocked on doors across Tucson to ask people to put out "We Stand With Rosa" yard signs.

The third trajectory was helping to build a grassroots faith movement to stop deportations. We learned from and shared with other sanctuary congregations; we met with hundreds of people who came in groups to learn about our work; and we did everything we could to support the sixteen other sanctuary cases that have occurred since our declaration in May, 2014.

After 461 days of prayer and organizing, Rosa safely left sanctuary after we reached an agreement with the government. And we rejoiced!

In 461 days we learned a lot – from how to sustain daily prayer vigils to recruiting volunteers to the ins and outs of our terribly complicated immigration system. But more than anything, we learned what a gift the work of sanctuary can be. We realized that we don't find true solidarity in the moments when the work is easy, but rather in the moments when we don't know if we have any hope left. After these 461 days, we are more than ever convinced that in this particular historical moment, the work of sanctuary is the faithful response of those who hear the words of scriptures, "For I was a stranger and you welcomed me." As millions of people around the globe run for their lives, sanctuary is a unique gift the faith community has to offer a world trying to decide whether to choose fear of the other or love of the stranger.

The Empire would like us to choose fear. After all, the business of Empire is the manufacturing and marketing of fear: fear that what we have is not enough and that there is someone out there who will arrive at our door and take from us not only our much cherished quality of life but our life itself. And once this fear takes root in our hearts and minds, the Empire

> **The business of Empire is the manufacturing and marketing of fear.**

convinces us that we need a bigger and stronger military, we need war, we need prisons, we need walls and more walls — around our homes, around our communities, and around our nation. Within this empire of fear, love of the stranger is anathema.

At Southside, we believe that we are called to be a people of faith who proclaim the radical love of Jesus Christ within this empire of fear and anxiety. We believe that within a context of increasing acts of violence and a narrative of fear of the other, whether it be workers from Mexico or refugees from Syria, the only antidote to fear is not more walls, not more security, but more love, for the only real secure community is the beloved community. In the midst of these anxious, contentious and fearful times, for better or worse, we chose love.

-AH

A Church of The Third Slave
Rick Ufford-Chase

From 2004 to 2006, I served as Moderator of the General Assembly of the Presbyterian Church (USA). I often describe the position as "temporary Pope with no power," as a frame of reference for those from other traditions. For two years I traveled 25 days or more each month, visiting churches in 128 of our 173 Presbyteries, nearly all fifty states, and thirteen countries around the world. I responded to any invitation to learn about ministry focused on justice and peacemaking. Many of those invitations were to visit projects that were carried out ecumenically and even in interfaith contexts. What surprised me, perhaps more than anything else during that experience, was my growing love for the church. In community after community, in the United States and around the world, I saw people of faith and religious conviction who were caring for the poor, advocating for justice, and taking significant risks for the cause of peace in their communities. Slowly, I began to appreciate the dilemma we confront as people of faith in the heart of the Empire: we long to be faithful even as we remain beholden to dominant cultural values that are antithetical to the most fundamental principles in our sacred text.

Christian churches across the United States are full of good people. In church after church, our members provide care for the elderly, sick, and homeless both within and outside of our own congregations. We show up when a natural disaster or crisis hits. We refuse to use hate speech, and we call out others when they do so. We believe in basic fairness. Most of us strive to build lives that cohere to our proclaimed values. These are the distinctive marks of what it has meant to be good Christians for decades, but they will not be enough as we confront the challenge of being the church in the United States in the coming years.

Years ago, when I first started my work as a young adult Mission Volunteer on the U.S./Mexico border, I took a group to meet with the representative for the Border Patrol office in Tucson. The agent disarmed all of us with his good humor and his willingness to talk about the challenges inherent in our nation's immigration enforcement. He said more than once that he was "just doing his job" and that he wished Congress would change our immigration laws. He reminded me of people in the church where I had grown up – the kind of person with whom I might have enjoyed going to a cookout.

After the meeting, our group went to Southside Presbyterian Church to meet with Rev. John Fife, Alison Harrington's predecessor. I was just getting to know John, but he was to become my pastor for the next twenty years. I explained that I felt kind of torn about my interaction with the agent because he was so likeable. John brought me up short. "You might as well figure it out now, Rick," John said:

> The evil that we confront in our time is not "bad people." In fact, I don't know anyone who gets up each morning thinking about how they can screw up the world. The real evil in our time, the one we have to watch out for, is what happens to good people who allow themselves to be co-opted into bad organizations or systems that oppress others. Every one of us is caught in that bind. Some of us spend our lives resisting it, others seem totally unaware, and still others actually make our livelihood by carrying out the mechanisms of those institutions that oppress people.

I've never forgotten that lesson, learned nearly thirty years ago. As I have spent time in churches across the U.S., I've become convinced that it sums up the challenge to the Church – especially the Church in the United States – in our time. We are a church dedicated to a gospel of liberation for people who are oppressed, while simultaneously co-opted by our existence within a project of Empire as great as any the world has ever known. What once seemed controversial in many of our seminaries now is taught as incontrovertible: Jesus was clearly a threat to the Roman Empire that dominated the lives of the People of Israel in first century Palestine. The gospel story leads inevitably to Jesus' death on the cross at the hands of that Empire.

In an attempt to rationalize the discord between Jesus' radical message of resistance in the gospel and our lives of complicity in the Empire of our time, we have obscured the meaning of many of our favorite stories in scripture. A message of political defiance and resistance to the Empire that would have been impossible to miss for both the Jews and the Gentiles of first century Palestine becomes a story of the power of God to offer personal transformation and salvation for those of us living in the midst of Empire in our own time. We have become adept at interpreting scripture in such a way as to water down the teachings and the life of Jesus, often turning its meaning upside down in the interest of finding congruence in the face of biblical values that are largely incongruent with the way we live our lives.

In the 25th chapter of the Gospel according to Matthew, Jesus tells three stories. After the story Jesus tells about the bridesmaids who weren't prepared, in which he warns the reader to watch out because something important is about to happen, he follows it with the story I grew up calling "The Parable of the Talents."

For it is as if a man, going on a journey, summoned his slaves..." the parable begins. Note that unlike the story of the bridesmaids that precedes it, this story does not begin as a traditional allegory with the words "the kingdom of heaven is like..." Instead, it appears to describe the way things really were in Jesus' time. However, most Christians I know were raised on the story as another allegory for the kingdom of heaven. That reading always confounded me as a child hearing it in Sunday School or preached from the pulpit. We are told that a wealthy landowner (presumably God, as I was raised on it) gathers before him three trusted slaves and gives them varying amounts of his personal estate to manage during what will apparently be a long absence. To one slave he gives five talents, to another two, and to the third, one. Upon his return, the first and second slaves report that they have doubled their master's money, and the affirmation from the master could not be more positive, *"Well done, good and trustworthy slave. You have been trustworthy in a few things, I will put you in charge of many things. Enter into the joy of your master."*

The third slave, however, reports *"Master, I knew you were a harsh man, reaping where you did not sow, and gathering where you did not scatter seed; so I was afraid, and I went and hid your money in the ground. Here you have what is yours."*

The master replies in a way anyone who has ever had to report failure to a harsh taskmaster would immediately recognize. *"Take the talent from him,"* the master says, and throw him into the outer darkness where there will be weeping and gnashing of teeth." Just to be sure no one will miss the point, Jesus reports that the man also states the obvious – *"for to all those who have, more will be given, and they will have an abundance, and for those who have nothing, even what they have will be taken away."*

The message is obvious, I learned, from my place of privilege in the Presbyterian Church. "We must employ our God given talents in a way that pleases God." But it never felt right to me. Why would God be portrayed as a harsh man, reaping where God has put no effort, and gathering where God has not prepared the soil? And why would this God respond to the third slave with a temper tantrum in which he is banished from the community? It wasn't until I was well into my twenties, attending a Bible study led by colleagues from the Evangelical Center for Pastoral Studies in Guatemala, that I realized how poorly I understood the meaning of the text.

"This is not an allegory for the Kingdom of Heaven," they insisted. "This is a parable about the way things really were in first century Palestine."

Wealthy landowners accumulated vast land holdings by making loans at exorbitant interest rates. Small farmers toiled to own their land outright, but they were beholden to wealthy creditors who charged impossible rates of interest. When the farmers couldn't pay, the wealthy men repossessed the lands and added them to their own holdings, which were so large they had to travel for months at a time to oversee them all. A talent was the equivalent of fifteen years' wage for a common laborer, so entrusting the first slave with five talents implied a lifetime of earnings.

This is a classic example of a text that has been re-interpreted to fit our understanding of ourselves as people of God. It's not about using the abilities God has given us to God's glory (however worthy that exercise might be), it is about the wealthy doubling their money on the backs of the poor. When we read the story through the eyes of the third slave, he becomes a hero who overcame his fear of an unjust master and found the courage to refuse to participate in the corrupt practices that would further impoverish his neighbors. In the end, he suffered the greatest consequence. Where the first two slaves were invited to enter into the economy of the privileged, "sharing in the joy of his master," the third slave was banished from that community of privilege and had everything – every last thing – stripped away from him.

Read in this way, this story becomes a critically important lesson in what it will take to live faithfully in the midst of Empire. Though most of us are not the masters who control the workings of a global economy designed to impoverish the vast majority of the world's people in order to provide unimaginable wealth to a relative handful of people, we are very much like the trusted slaves who are given a choice to participate in "reaping where we do not sow, and gathering where we do not scatter seed." Like the third slave, we live with the real fear that if we question the system, we too may end up with nothing.

This dilemma is not new to us. Since Constantine made Christianity the religion of the State, Christians have repeatedly found ourselves in the awkward position of using a liberation text written for a people on the margins of their society as the justification for blessing the Empire. Christianity provided the theological justification for the conquest and genocide of indigenous peoples and the theft of their land. Christianity blessed the colonizers in insisting that they had not just a *right* but a *moral obligation* to wage war – militarily and economically – against anyone who did not profess belief in Jesus Christ. Many Christians across the U.S. today find theological justification for the border enforcement strategy confronted by Alison Harrington and the members of Southside Presbyterian Church in Arizona. Mark Adams, a colleague of Alison's who lives and works in the border cities of Douglas, Arizona, and Agua Prieta, Sonora, describes the policy this way:

> *For 150 years, a fluid border existed between the U.S. and Mexico, but in the early 1990's, policy makers in the United States chose to implement a much more robust, costly and deadly border policy. The U.S. Government decided to step up to control our border in a time when NAFTA has exacerbated the economic push and pull from Mexico to the U.S. With Operation Hold the Line in El Paso and Operation Gatekeeper in San Diego, the Border Patrol has effectively closed traditional crossing points for undocumented migration into the U.S. and rerouted them to less populated, and more dangerous, areas. In the late 1990s and early 2000s, we forced people through the deserts to Agua Prieta, Sonora and the adjacent town of Douglas, Arizona. By the mid- and late- 2000s, we pushed the flow of migration to even more remote and deadly areas, like the deserts and mountains east of Yuma and the Altar Valley, southwest of Tucson.*

> *Doris Meissner, who headed the Immigration and Naturalization Service during the Clinton administration and oversaw the initial creation and implementation of a massive border build-up, stated that we would use mountains and deserts as "lethal deterrents" to stop undocumented migration. She was half right—our change in policy did turn out to be lethal.*

Since the inception of Operation Gatekeeper in 1994, more than 6,500 men, women and children have died crossing the U.S./Mexico border—more than two times the number of persons who died in the attacks of 9/11. More people have perished trying to reach the "American Dream" than the combined number of U.S. soldiers who died in the Iraq and Afghanistan wars.

Mark's stories from the borderlands unmask the reality of Empire. Nowhere is the real cost of the Empire project as clear as it is on the border where the Empire claims to be defending itself as it defines who is "in" and who is "out." The greater the economic power and political hegemony of the Empire, the more it must defend its borders with automatic weapons, tens of thousands of border patrol agents, steel walls and a sophisticated, high-tech security system that can determine in an instant whom it deems to be a threat.

In the midst of the militarization of the border as Mark describes, I heard a Congressman from Colorado being interviewed on a national talk radio program. When the Congressman announced that he was a Christian, the host asked him how he reconciled his support for this policy with the same scripture from Leviticus that Alison referenced in her essay - that we must welcome the stranger in our land. His answer took my breath away. "I absolutely believe that we must welcome any person *with documents*," he explained. Without hesitation, he completely redefined the meaning of the text, and he may not have been fully aware he was doing so.

The exchange caricatured the dilemma we confront as Christians living in an empire that was supposedly built on Christian values but in actual fact often stands in direct contradiction to the teachings of Jesus. The bad news – for the good people of the church - is that we swim in this water. That is to say, we barely notice the inconsistency between the values we profess and the way we live. Few of us who have been born and raised in the dominant culture and religion of the United States can imagine that God has not ordained and blessed our way of life. We are the ultimate example of what John Fife was talking about – good people trying to do the right thing in a system that is inherently sinful and designed to bring down death upon anyone who threatens it, while fundamentally unaware of the moral bankruptcy of the system itself. If you think that seems hyperbolic, I invite you to read Alison's essay again, for Southside is a church that long ago opened its eyes to this reality, and it has truly counted the cost of standing in resistance to the Empire.

Lest we think that the borderlands are an anomaly, I should hasten to add that the vagaries of the Empire project are readily apparent to those who aren't full citizens, whomever and wherever they may be. These vagaries are evident in communities of people of color in the U.S., and they are evident in those places long colonized by the Empire around the world. Colonization – so hard to see from the position of privilege in the Empire – is an ever-present and obvious reality to the colonized. Undocumented immigrants, so-called "minority populations" in the United States, workers in the U.S. who have lost their jobs to the global economy, those who have experienced the cradle-to-prison pipeline, Mexicans and Central Americans displaced from their land as a result of Free Trade Agreements designed to benefit multinational agribusiness corporations, those displaced by war: the list is long of those on the underside of the Empire project who have a visceral understanding of the reality faced by the Third Slave.

In the summer of 2015, I attended a workshop where I was introduced to the concept of "decoloniality." A growing number of activists, scholars and theologians are making the case that people whose central project has historically been to colonize the other must actively work to deconstruct, or "decolonize" our minds, and our educational institutions, and our faith. The language captivated me, and I find myself trying it on more and more. What might it look like for the church to enter into an intentional process of decolonizing our faith? The colonized mind is one that can comprehend only "the water we swim in" as an Empire people, unable to imagine how this project could not be as good for everyone else as it is for us. It's "just the way things are," and few of us can summon the moral courage and creativity to imagine the world working any differently.

But what if we could?

The good news – which we who are followers of Jesus actually call "Good News" – is that Jesus taught and ministered in a similar situation. He was a part of a religious tradition that dated back hundreds of years with strands of justice woven throughout, and he sought to call out the easy comfort that tradition had found with the Roman Empire, the greatest empire his world had ever known, just as today ours is currently the greatest empire ever known.

What if Christians returned to our sacred texts, the ones with which we grew up, for a second look? What if our churches committed to the project of decolonizing our faith? What if we turned to people like Alison Harrington and Mark Adams, who have intentionally placed themselves on the outer edges of the Empire project, where there really is disconsolate weeping and the unresolved rage that Jesus called "gnashing of teeth?" Is it possible for a church that has been in the heart of Empire for as long as we have to make a course correction and move intentionally from the center of the Empire to the margins?

Our faith requires us to practice resistance. For the church in the United States, this is the fundamental challenge of our time. Failure to faithfully resist guarantees our irrelevance and demise as an institution, or worse, our continued existence – but only as sycophants to Caesar. The Bible is replete with stories of God's disappointment in our lack of faithfulness as God's people. Further, God is clearly unafraid to let us lose everything when we are unable to summon the courage to be faithful in the face of great cost. If we don't have that courage, we have no right to call ourselves people of God.

But it is also true that God delights in us when we discover the capacity to resist the forces of domination and oppression and death. Mark Adams describes just such an experience:

As the number of deaths increased, a small group of folks began gathering just north of the U.S. port of entry every Tuesday for a prayer vigil. Catholics, Presbyterians, Quakers, Mennonites, Episcopalians and other people of conscience remembered those who lost their lives. We prayed for their families and our governments, that we might find a better way. We prayed to encourage one another in the hard work of witness, service and struggle for change. The first few times, as we marched with the south-bound traffic toward the Mexican port of entry, law enforcement mobilized with vehicles, guns and cameras to hold what seemed to be a counter vigil.

Following a particularly intense encounter after a prayer vigil in front of the Border Patrol Station, we began to meet with the local station chief to express our outrage over the combination of economic and political forces that were leading to a surge in deaths. I asked the station chief if he thought that the policy that he upholds – a policy that we agreed led to higher risk, more smuggling, increased suffering, and overwhelming death – was a moral one. He responded, "There's God's law and there's man's [sic] law and sometimes they come into conflict with one another. I am sworn to uphold man's law. For you, there is no higher authority than God, but for me, there is no higher authority than the U.S. Constitution."

With that, he succinctly summarized the conflict I was uncovering. My faith was drawing me into a confrontation with Empire.

I feel it too - the sense that we who follow Jesus have no choice. There is no greater calling than to live faithfully in challenging times, and most of the Biblical stories we remember about the people of God are the stories of those who have overcome their fear and followed God into a new thing.

To write the next chapter of faithfulness in resistance to the project of Empire: what could be more thrilling than that?

-RUC

Discussion Questions:

1. Mark Adams described the system of border enforcement as an example of the anti-biblical tendencies of Empire. Can you think of examples of the Empire project in your own community?

2. Alison wrote *"And for us, the only way to be church within this Empire is to enact love in ways that disrupt the machinery of the Empire."* What do you think she means?

3. Rick described his intrigue with the idea of "decolonizing our faith." What does this mean to you?

4. Rick asserts that the failure to faithfully resist the power of Empire guarantees our irrelevance and demise as an institution. Do you think he is right about that? Why or why not?

Chapter 2
Dismantling White Supremacy

Black. Lives. Matter.
Annanda Barclay

I sometimes struggle when talking with white people about racism and how it functions, because I feel like I'm trying to explain how to breathe to another human. Our bodies already participate in the breathing process. We are inhaling and exhaling without thought. How do I share an awareness of breath when one is already breathing? I don't quite know what to say that will trigger the 'Aha!' moment, bringing others into that awareness that is so clear to me because of my lived identities. For too long, we have heard too many stories in the news of black people being murdered in disproportionate numbers by the police or white vigilantes. These stories have become as normal a part of life as those breaths we take.

Black Lives Matter is the current era in the continuum of the civil rights movement. The media primarily focuses on BLM's response to the deaths of black people due to police murder, but the movement is far more extensive than that. Just like the US Civil Rights movement of the 20th century, and the Abolitionist movement before that, this is an invitational movement that acts like a canary in a coal mine; warning us of the danger we are currently experiencing as a church and society. For all these reasons BLM is fundamentally relevant to the church and our discipleship as Christians.

How the church interacts, ignores, embraces, and denies people of color is a reflection of how the church participates in the violence of racism. For the most part, I do not believe the church currently makes a conscious effort to be racist. However, to use my own home, the Presbyterian Church, as an example, we must take into serious consideration: our lack of black pastors in general, let alone as heads of staff in congregations; our token black people or families in the pews (if we have any in our congregations at all); and the consistently understood identity of the denomination as inherently white. Many of our local, national, and international mission projects consist of "helping" communities of color. All these things exemplify how the church, although well-intentioned and made up of good, kind, loving people, participates in perpetuating racism. All too often, historical Presbyterian congregations of color are forgotten or erased within their local presbyteries and new congregations of color are tokenized as trophies of church growth.

In early childhood I was raised in an historically African-American Presbyterian church on Chicago's southwest side. I remember white people in our church only one time, and that was when a group of young adult volunteers stayed at our church to do mission work in the neighborhood. Later, in my early teen years, my understanding of what it means to be Presbyterian was expanded. My family moved to Georgia, and we were one of two black families in our church. This church became the family that loved and raised me just as my church in Chicago had. The difference I experienced can be summed up in two words, access and culture. In Georgia, I became aware of the important role of the Presbytery, the cultural significance of the Montreat Conference Center and youth trips. Both churches were similar in terms of numbers of active members, but it was clear the access and opportunity that I had and experienced at my predominately white church in Georgia was drastically different from anything I experienced or was even aware of existing in Chicago. It was truly a difference of night and day.

This example parallels my daily normalized experience of structural racism. It parallels the distinct historical meta-narrative of the black south side and central-north side white neighborhoods in Chicago. Both neighborhoods are a part of the broader community of Chicago. However, black neighborhoods in the south side cannot look to their police or local government for security or equal access and participation in all the city has to offer. The white central and north neighborhoods, however, can. Culturally, those north and central white neighborhoods, just like the church that raised me in Georgia, don't have to worry about representation, their children being shot or not having access to a great education. However, the church that raised me in my early childhood, along with the neighborhood in which it's located, has to worry about lack of access to jobs, healthcare, public transit, a police force and local government that are not really looking out for their safety, and a presbytery that needs to do better in giving them access and representation to the larger assembly.

The BLM movement is appropriately confronting predominantly white denominations like mine. Yes, this confrontation is a threat, but only to white supremacy. This literal crying out is only a threat to that which continues to prevent the church from living into Christ's gospel with greater integrity, and being a loving neighbor to people of color. BLM provides an invitation to participate in the reconciliation and mending of the complex and insidious institutional violence that is white supremacy, made manifest in racism.

The hierarchical system of race creates an inherent inequality of the worthiness of a human being, based on white supremacy. Notice, I say human being, because I firmly believe white supremacy and racism oppresses white people as well. The idea that whiteness is inherently better automatically creates a false sense of entitlement, control, power, and even a false sense of godly righteousness. All of these prevent us from recognizing that the systemic attempt to control black bodies is not a healthy form of self-love or self-preservation. It is a relationship that abuses one's neighbor instead of loving them.

In our society, this embedded inequality justifies the mass criminalization of black people, the zoning in big cities and small towns that creates the conditions of the ghetto, the unequal opportunities for jobs, and the murder of people of color by police and vigilantes. In the church, it justifies only referencing white biblical scholars and theologians in the pulpit and classroom, or not calling a black pastor. It justifies using MLK references and painfully ironic singing of spiritual hymns in February, and calling it enough. It divorces us from the ability to comprehend black people as neighbors who are living and ministering alongside us, not merely communities to be ministered to.

Reform always comes from the margins.

Reform always comes from the margins. It occurs where mainstream society benefits from the status quo at the expense of the "othered". Black Lives Matter is calling us to empathize and cry out in solidarity regarding the injustices against black people. The movement is reminiscent, in many ways, of the prophets from Hebrew Scripture through whom the Spirit speaks. BLM exists because we have failed in our ability to live out the second greatest tenet of our discipleship, to love your neighbor as oneself. Racism, though systemic, has always been about relationship between neighbors. Christ reveals to us that how we are in relationship with ourselves has a direct impact on how we interact with other people, and how we live into our discipleship.

BLM is calling for an end to the abusive relationship of white supremacy to which we are all currently bound. It is crying out, love! Love! Love! Love! We must find the roots of our humanity so we can see black people in their pain. Black people must also find the roots of their humanity to continue to acknowledge our own dignity, worth and self-love, and not succumb to bitterness and hate. As part of finding those roots, BLM calls out to the mainstream black community to love the non-heterosexual members and women and trans and gender-nonconforming people whose existence in the black community has been historically ignored or met with violence.

We must love ourselves and, in doing so, reveal our inner courage by facing the unknown without fear. We must reject our craving for a false sense of power and entitlement, and have the courage to speak out and act on our conviction. As Christians, we are called to do this rooted in the truth that we are all made in the image of God, and are all worthy to be treated with grace and love.

God has gifted us with multiple identities in a singular body. We can define ourselves by age, biological sex, race, nationality, ability, sexuality, gender identity and expression, socio-economic status, education, addiction status, and so on. Claiming one identity does not negate our other identities. Identities are neither negative or positive, they simply are. These various identities bring the gifts needed to dismantle racism. It's time we acknowledge these intersections of identities as gifts that reveal our full humanity in relationships. What a beautiful gift! Each of us is more than one thing, or even a collection of identifying labels. Each of us is "other" in different parts of our lives. This is how our intersectional identities work as the essential tools needed to empathize and break the well-intentioned, but all too common, patterns of guilt, complacency, and comfort. Those patterns perpetuate racism far more than a hate group like the KKK. Guilt, shame, complacency, and comfort act as emotional and physical barriers inhibiting our ability to create change. White people aren't bad. White supremacy is bad!

The work of dismantling white supremacy will not be easy. It will be uncomfortable. It will be hard. There will be mistakes made along the way. It is the road less traveled, but the reward will be shalom. We must find the roots in our humanity so we don't participate in reinforcing racial violence, but in ending it. Let us hear the cry of our sibling's blood from the ground, and respond in anger, pain and empathy. Hope is not lost. It does not have to be this way, it never had to be this way. There is still time to change. Let us recognize this ability to change within ourselves. Take courage in the hard path ahead, and embrace it with warm and loving hearts. All these things are steps toward dismantling white supremacy from the foundation.

-AB

The Fight For the Soul of the Church
Rick Ufford-Chase

Here's the problem: the system of white supremacy works for me. It's not in my self-interest to challenge it. When public schools weren't working for my own kids, I had the choice to send them to a private school, and I took it in spite of all the things I have believed for most of my adult life about the importance of committing to public schools that afford equal access to a quality education for everyone. I used all kinds of mitigating circumstances to try to justify the decisions my wife and I made, but at the end of the day, what was undeniable was the access that I had because of the color of my skin.

I have access to generational wealth that it is extremely unlikely a black or brown person in the United States will have. I have never been at risk of not being able to find a job that offers a secure paycheck, in large measure because of the privileges I have enjoyed as a white person. Even more remarkable, it's hard for me to imagine not being able to find meaningful work that allows me to follow my passions and pursue my interests. My wife and I own a house, and I have a cabin on land my mother grew up on in the mountains of Vermont. If something bad were to happen in my community that would threaten my family's health (such as public officials knowingly poisoning the water system as we've just discovered they did in Flint, Michigan), I have no doubt that I would have the resources either to ensure my family's safety or to move away from that "at-risk" community to protect them. I can continue to list the privileges that I have and have refused to give up, but it would be a very, very long list that would touch upon every aspect of my life.

Though more difficult to examine or to quantify in any meaningful way, I also pay a significant cost for the unearned privilege that I enjoy. Once I began to consciously locate myself in solidarity with communities of people who do not enjoy my same privilege, the dissonance between the teachings of the gospel that I profess and the privilege that I enjoy became inescapable, and the result is a steady eating away of my soul. I believe that the spiritual cost of that dissonance is actually quite high, though I hesitate to write the words for fear of how silly they will appear to people who do not benefit from the privilege of whiteness.

There is also the cost of separateness, a sense that no matter what I do to try to address this fundamental inequity, I quite likely will never overcome the barriers that have been carefully constructed to keep me separate from those who do not enjoy my privileges in the system of white supremacy. It may not be possible for me to ever experience the fullness of what Jesus described as the kingdom of God, or what Mark Lomax and other theologians have renamed the "kin-dom" of God, or what Dr. King referred to as "the Beloved Community."

The truth is, I've been raised to believe that such notions of community are naïve, and perhaps even irresponsible. The culture in which I was raised highly prized independence and rugged individualism, and the white world compounded those spoils when it taught me that I should always aim for complete self-sufficiency. We see the need to depend on one another as weakness, and this is a fundamental problem for our churches today.

We say we want community. In my judgment we are totally dependent on radical expressions of community to resist the challenges of a system of Empire and white supremacy. Though these desires are deeply embedded in our biblical traditions, it is also true that there are huge impediments to actually creating communities like the ones that the Apostle Paul tried to nurture, where there is neither Jew nor Greek, male nor female, master nor slave. This task confronts and confounds the church, and it is so daunting as to appear impossible.

First Presbyterian Church of York, the church in which I grew up, did so much to try to follow the gospel. At a time when segregation was still very much alive and well in communities across the north and the south, the congregations of First and Faith Presbyterian Churches (an historically black church) defied deeply ingrained racial prejudice and firmly entrenched racism to unite as one body. Given what was going in the Civil Rights Movement in 1965, that defiance was no small thing. Further, First Presbyterian made overt attempts to genuinely welcome the members of Faith into full participation in the life of the larger, white congregation. But this merged church community also presents a case study in just how high the bar is and how impossible the task confronting us may be. In the summer of 1968, less than three years after the two churches merged, and two months before my family moved to York so that my father could join the pastoral staff there, "racial unrest" began to make itself known in this small city. It appears to have started with the arrests of a group of young black men for breaking curfew (a law later proven to have been unfairly enforced), and quickly became nightly conflicts between the police, the African-American community, and gangs of young white men who escalated the violence. Keep in mind, "race riots" (which today we would call protests) were taking place in cities all across the United States at that time.

A year later, and less than a year into my father's ministry with the youth program, the conflict again escalated when a young, white Police Officer, Henry Schaad, was shot by a black protester as he patrolled the streets in an armored vehicle. His wounds would prove to be fatal within a few weeks. The next night, on July 18th, a young African-American woman from South Carolina named Lilly Belle Allen was visiting family members in York. When their car made a wrong turn and ended up in a white neighborhood, a group of young men fired shots at the car and Lilly Belle Allen was killed. No one was convicted in either of these shootings until the District Attorney re-opened the cases following an investigative story by the York Daily Record more than thirty years later.

Here's what I can't get my head around: For all the power of the witness made by First and Faith Presbyterian churches with their merger in 1965, I can find no record of First Presbyterian Church acknowledging or responding to the clearly racially-motivated violence three years later. My father himself remembers little beyond the characterization of the unrest as "riots when the National Guard rolled down the streets in tanks," in spite of the reality that the events took place within six or eight blocks of the church. I have to imagine that African-American members of the church were gravely concerned about the shootings, because most – if not all – of them lived within the city and in close proximity to the violence.

In December of 2015 I visited the church for the fiftieth anniversary of the merger. I sat near the front of the sanctuary I had grown up in with two African-American women who had seen a poster that the Warren Cooper Jazz Ensemble would be doing a concert and had come to hear him, though neither of them were members of the church. After I introduced myself, the conversation quickly and logically turned to the topics of race, racism, and the system of white supremacy, all of which was language with which the women were fluent and comfortable. When I asked what they knew of the summer of 1969, both immediately knew Lilly Belle Allen's name and could recount the story of what had taken place, though neither of them actually lived in York at that time.

So how is it that I was raised in a multiracial church and never once heard these stories between 1968 (when I was four) and 1985, when my father took another parish and my family left the community? The answer, I think, is that this congregation did so much that was right in terms of welcoming people into their community, but then did not make fundamental changes to address the cultural and racial dynamics of the newly merged congregations. Worship stayed the same, Christian Education stayed the same, and the question of what was considered "polite conversation" does not appear to have changed. The congregation does not appear to have felt called to address the crisis that was taking place in their community any differently because they had black members, and there is no mention I have been able to discover in the public record of the pastoral staff showing up to work with African-American pastors in the city to address the violence.

I love this church for the ways in which it showed courage and for the ways I was shaped because of it. First Presbyterian Church of York, Pennsylvania, stands for all of us who are white and "progressive" in our thinking about race. It represents the best of who we have been as a denomination that is 92-percent white and steeped in the reality of privilege associated with being white, Protestant, economically advantaged, and supposedly well-educated. It highlights the fundamental problem we confront – that we are still largely unaware of the ways in which we ourselves are the beneficiaries of a system of white supremacy that offers us significant privilege that is not accessible to most other people.

Our failure to address fundamental questions of racism, white privilege and a system of white supremacy that remain deeply entrenched in our church and in our society is, at root, a failure to be faithful to the gospel. It is a structural reality that actually impedes our ability to be church. It is a time for all of us to embrace Dr. King's vision – Jesus' vision – of the Beloved Community.

> **Our failure to address fundamental questions of racism...is, at root, a failure to be faithful to the gospel.**

Annanda Barclay's description of the Black Lives Matter movement makes it clear that this is a rich and complex part of the broader, decades-long Civil Rights movement. It offers an opportunity to enter into a significant conversation as allies to people who are trying to get to the heart of a system that has worked against them for generations. Here's how Claudia Rankine describes the reorientation we will need to become a people who can be genuine allies in this movement, in an article titled "The Condition of Black Life is Mourning," published by the *New York Times Magazine* in the summer of 2015[1]:

> *I asked another friend what it's like being the mother of a black son. "The condition of black life is one of mourning," she said bluntly. For her, mourning lived in real time inside her and her son's reality: At any moment she might lose her reason for living. Though the white liberal imagination likes to feel temporarily bad about black suffering, there really is no mode of empathy that can replicate the daily strain of knowing that as a black person you can be killed for simply being black: no hands in your pockets, no playing music, no sudden movements, no driving your car, no walking at night, no walking in the day, no turning onto this street, no*

---

[1] Claudia Rankine, "The Condition of Black Life is Mourning," *New York Times*, June 22, 2015.

entering this building, no standing your ground, no standing here, no standing there, no talking back, no playing with toy guns, no living while black.

And now juxtapose Claudia's words with this excerpt from "White Debt," an equally powerful essay by Eula Bliss, published later that year by the same magazine[2]:

Sitting with [Claudia Rankine's] essay in front of me after the Charleston church massacre, I asked myself what the condition of white life might be. I wrote "complacence" on a blank page. Hearing the term "white supremacist" in the wake of that shooting had given me another occasion to wonder whether white supremacists are any more dangerous than regular white people, who tend to enjoy supremacy without believing in it. After staring at "complacence" for quite a long time, I looked it up and discovered that it didn't mean exactly what I thought it meant. "A feeling of smug or uncritical satisfaction with oneself or one's achievements" might be an apt description of the dominant white attitude, but that's more active than what I had in mind. I thought "complacence" meant sitting there in your house, neither smug nor satisfied, just lost in the illusion of ownership. This is an illusion that depends on forgetting the redlining, block-busting, racial covenants, contract buying, loan discrimination, housing projects, mass incarceration, predatory lending and deed thefts that have prevented so many black Americans from building wealth the way so many white Americans have, through homeownership. I erased "complacence" and wrote "complicity." I erased it. "Debt," I wrote. Then, "forgotten debt."

---

[2] Eula Bliss, "White Debt," *New York Times*, December 6, 2015.

And from later in the same article by Eula Bliss. . .

> . . . Once you've been living in a house for a while, you tend to begin to believe that it's yours, even though you don't own it yet. When those of us who are convinced of our own whiteness deny our debt, this may be an inevitable result of having lived for so long in a house bought on credit but never paid off. We ourselves have never owned slaves, we insist, and we never say the n-word. "It is as though we have run up a credit-card bill," Ta-Nehisi Coates writes of Americans, "and, having pledged to charge no more, remain befuddled that the balance does not disappear."

These two remarkable authors pose a huge challenge to the church. Are we interested in creating a community in which we can affirm more than one cultural reality and make space for more than one kind of work? Can our churches become a place of mourning – the kind of mourning that is grounded not in naïve grief that has no desire to know how we are complicit in the tragedy, but instead in a grief that recognizes our responsibility for a system of domination based on skin color, in which we all are participants and for which we all bear some responsibility?

And, can our churches become places where we commit to truth-telling and offer ourselves up to an unflinching and faith-filled commitment to become communities of resistance? Can we model a different way of being?

This pivotal question confronts the church. Forgotten debt robs all of us – black, white, Native American, Latino, Asian, Caribbean, African, multiracial together – condemning us all to a system of white supremacy that will assure another generation in which Black Lives Really Don't Matter.

Claudia Rankine describes why this is the fundamental civil rights question of our time.

> *"The Black Lives Matter movement can be read as an attempt to keep mourning an open dynamic in our culture because black lives exist in a state of precariousness. Mourning then bears both the vulnerability inherent in black lives and the instability regarding a future for those lives. Unlike earlier black-power movements that tried to fight or segregate for self-preservation, Black Lives Matter aligns with the dead, continues the mourning and refuses the forgetting in front of all of us. If the Rev. Martin Luther King Jr.'s civil rights movement made demands that altered the course of American lives and backed up those demands with the willingness to give up your life in service of your civil rights, with Black Lives Matter, a more internalized change is being asked for: recognition."*

Can we become that kind of church? Can we respond to the prophets who call us back from the moral abyss in our time just as the prophet Amos called the people of Israel back from that abyss in his own? Can our church re-create itself as the Apostle Paul imagined it, where the distinction of privilege has fallen away? Can we embrace not only Dr. King's beautiful image of the beloved community but also the hard work he insisted upon that moves to an entirely new way of being in relationship with one another? Can we, as in Annanda's vision, see Black Lives Matter as an opportunity to truly become the church?

- This will be a Confessional church – a church that unflinchingly confesses its complicity and its access to privilege every single week without rationalization.

- This will be a church of solidarity, which moves out and takes risks to stand with people who are working to address this reality.

- This will be a church willing to challenge its own privilege, and to model that every privilege we carry must be examined, and no privilege accepted without the insistence that it will be accorded to all of us and not just to some of us.

- This will be a church that makes space for more than one cultural expression, welcoming and protecting the heritage each of us bring to the table without succumbing to temptation of cultural appropriation nor insisting on homogenization into one community that pretends difference doesn't exist.

In short, this will be a church that embraces the intersectionality that Annanda and many activists in her generation are lifting up as the only acceptable way forward – a space where embracing one identity does not come at the expense of other identities that may be carried by the very same person or held by others in the same community.

For white people, and for a church dominated by white culture, this will be a hard row to hoe. As Eula Bliss wrote in her article:

> *Refusing to collude in injustice is, I've found, easier said than done. Collusion is written onto our way of life, and nearly every interaction among white people is an invitation to collusion. Being white is easy, in that nobody is expected to think about being white, but this is exactly what makes me uneasy about it. Without thinking, I would say that believing I am white doesn't cost me anything, that it's pure profit, but I suspect that isn't true. I suspect whiteness is costing me, as [James] Baldwin would say, my moral life.*

I find Ms. Bliss's words deeply compelling. In the context of the church, it makes me think that how the church navigates our collusion in the system of white supremacy is a struggle for our soul, and the failure to do so is likely to cost us our moral life. After several decades of personal anti-racism work and working to create intentional anti-racist spaces, I am not clear that the white church has it in us to be this honest, to take this level of risk, and to let go of the benefits we enjoy because white supremacy is real.

On the other hand, we are a part of a story that is built upon the notion that God is not done with us. Stories of personal transformation abound, and I believe in them. Each time we who are white manage to question our unearned privilege is a step in the right direction. Each moment we summon the courage to stand with those who do not carry that privilege and demand a change builds up the whole community. When our churches do a thoughtful inventory of the ways in which they support the system of white supremacy they are taking a step toward the Beloved Community, and I believe that it pleases God.

-RUC

Discussion Questions:

1. Annanda shared her experience of growing up in two different churches - one with access to the privileges associated with white supremacy, and the other without. Have you had personal experiences where you have noticed such differences? If not, why not?

2. Rick began with a confession of the clear ways in which he benefits from a system of white privilege that favors him. Share examples in your own life of access – or lack of access – to privilege based on the color of your skin.

3. Do you think that members of your faith community are prepared for this conversation? Why or why not?

4. The entire text from each of the two New York Magazine articles in 2015 that made such an impact on Rick are available here. Read the entire text of the articles and discuss what they bring up for you. This may take several weeks, but it's worth it.
    a. http://www.nytimes.com/2015/06/22/magazine/the-condition-of-black-life-is-one-of-mourning.html?_r=0 - Claudia Rankine
    b. http://www.nytimes.com/2015/12/06/magazine/white-debt.html - Eula Bliss

Chapter 3
Reimagining Ecological Theology

Watershed Discipleship
Ched Myers

It is impossible to overstate the depth and breadth of the social and ecological crises that have been stalking human civilization for centuries, and now arrived in the Anthropocene epoch. These interlocking catastrophes are backing us into an historical cul-de-sac. On the social side, they include intensifying economic disparity, wealth concentration, and racialized poverty; entrenched racial, ethnic, and religious balkanization and enmity; and the globalization of militarized politics. On the environmental side, they include climate catastrophe and carbon addiction; habitat destruction and species extinction; and resource exhaustion (so-called "peak everything").

Scientific assessments of this matrix of violence, injustice and unsustainability have converged in a grim consensus that the human project is well down the road of what Derrick Jensen calls an "Endgame"—whether or not those of us insulated by race, class or national or geographic privilege feel it yet existentially. Longtime environmental analyst James Speth provides a terse summary[1]:

> "How serious is the threat to the environment?
> Here is one measure of the problem: all we
> have to do to destroy the planet's climate and

---

[1] James Gustave Speth, *The Bridge at the Edge of the World: Capitalism, the Environment, and Crossing from Crisis to Stability* (Devon, PA: Caravan, 2008), x.

biota and leave a ruined world to our children and grandchildren is to keep doing exactly what we are doing today, with no growth in the human population or the world economy. Just continue to release greenhouse gases at the current rates, just continue to impoverish ecosystems and release toxic chemicals at current rates, and the world in the latter part of the century won't be fit to live in."

Elements of this sobering diagnosis are finally dawning on world leaders, from popes to presidents, particularly in the wake of the recent 2015 United Nations climate summit in Paris. At the turn of the millennium Worldwatch Institute's Ed Ayres poignantly called this historical ultimatum "God's Last Offer." Christian faith and practice from now on will unfold either in light of or in spite of these social and ecological crises: we must choose between discipleship or denial.

To be sure, environmental stewardship is arguably the fastest-growing expression of public concern in North American churches, initially among mainstream Catholics and Protestants but also, increasingly, evangelicals. But while the Creation Care trend has been a necessary corrective, it is not yet sufficient in its responses to the Creation crisis we now face everywhere. On one hand, prescriptive suggestions commended to congregations are too often merely cosmetic. "Going green" by recycling or light bulb changes—but avoiding political controversies such as Tar Sands extraction or mountaintop removal mining—does not lead toward the deep paradigm shifts with which churches need to wrestle. On the other hand, environmental theologies tend still to be either overly abstract, insufficiently radical in diagnosis, and/or not practically constructive. The church will embody a moral equivalent to these times neither by advocating for minor reforms nor by offering a new rhetorical lexicon. Rather, it needs to promote pastoral and theological disciplines which are radical, diagnosing the root pathologies within and around us while also drawing deeply on the roots of our faith traditions. Yet these must also be practical, empowering deliberate steps toward significant change. Our task as Christians is nothing less than working to help turn our history around—which is, as it happens, the meaning of the biblical discourse of repentance.

In 2017, Christians will commemorate the quincentenary of the Protestant Reformation, launched when Martin Luther famously proclaimed: "Here I stand, I can do no other." It is past time for a "new Reformation" in which our churches stand against ecocide and for a just and sustainable future. Such a groundswell has not developed to date in North America, however, because industrial culture has rendered most Christians unable to answer the question: "Where is the here upon which we take our stand?" We have been socialized to be more loyal to abstractions and superstructures than literate in the actual biosphere that sustains us; more adept at mobility than grounded in the bioregions in which we reside (but do not truly inhabit). And we have been too infected with functional Docetism to realize fully an incarnational faith.

> It is past time for a "new Reformation" in which our churches stand against ecocide and for a just and sustainable future.

Kentucky farmer Wendell Berry is one of the foremost Christian voices addressing placelessness in North America. More than a quarter century ago Berry argued – quite out of fashion – that "global thinking" was often merely a euphemism for abstract anxiety or passion that is useless in struggles to save real places. "The question that must be addressed," he contended, "is not how to care for the planet, but how to care for each of the planet's millions of human and natural neighborhoods, each of its millions of small pieces and parcels of land." Only love for specific places – what native Hawaiians call aloha 'aina – can motivate us to struggle on their behalf.

The focus for Christian theology, spirituality and politics in the 21st century, I believe, needs to be "re-place-ment." Over the last half century, a paradigm has been emerging that is placed and practical, radical yet constructive, contextual yet universal: bioregionalism. Kirkpatrick Sale's 1985 primer Dwellers in the Land: The Bioregional Vision provides a helpful definition: "Bio is from the Greek word for forms of life…and region is from the Latin *regere*, territory to be ruled…. They convey together a life-territory, a place defined by its life forms, its topography and its biota, rather than by human dictates; a region governed by nature, not legislature. And if the concept initially strikes us as strange, that may perhaps only be a measure of how distant we have become from the wisdom it conveys."

More recently, many bioregionalists, myself included, have emphasized an even more specific locus for re-inhabitory literacy and engagement, based on what is most basic to life: water. Wherever we reside – city, suburb, or rural area – our place is deeply intertwined within a larger system called a watershed, drained by a watercourse and its tributaries into a particular body of water such as a pond, lake or ocean. John Wesley Powell (the first non-indigenous person to run the Colorado River through the Grand Canyon in 1869) offered an enduring definition of a watershed as "that area of land, a bounded hydrologic system, within which all living things are inextricably linked by their common water course and where, as humans settled, simple logic demanded that they become part of the community." All of us live in a watershed, no matter how ignorant we may be about it (which most of us are).[2] It is there we must take our stand.

---

[2] Americans can locate theirs at http://cfpub.epa.gov/surf/locate/index.cfm

Permaculturist Brock Dolman asserts: "Watersheds underlie all human endeavors and form the foundation for all future aspirations and survival. The idea is one of a cradle," he says, cupping his hands into a little boat. "Your home basin of relations is your lifeboat." Our watersheds represent a community, he continued, "within which every living organism within this basin is interconnected and interdependent." This represents the most viable "geographic scale of applied sustainability, which must be regenerative because we desperately are in need of making up for lost time."

What would it mean for Christians to re-center our citizen-identity in the topography of Creation, rather than in the political geography of dominant cultural ideation, and to ground our discipleship practices in the watersheds in which we reside? A network of faith-rooted organizers and educators around North America are embracing an approach I call "watershed discipleship." It is an intentional triple entendre:

1. Recognizing that we are in a watershed historical moment of crisis, which demands that environmental and social justice and sustainability be integral to everything we do as inhabitants of specific places;

2. Acknowledging the bioregional locus of an incarnational following of Jesus: our discipleship and the life of the local church inescapably take place in a watershed context;

3. And implying that we need to be disciples of our watersheds, learning from and recovenanting with the local "Book of Creation."

The challenge, to paraphrase an argument made in 1968 by Senegalese environmentalist Baba Dioum, is that "we won't save places we don't love; we can't love places we don't know, and we don't know places we haven't learned."

From the beginning of human history, a symbiotic, relational ethos of watershed literacy and stewardship was crucial to the survival and flourishing of traditional societies. We have a long way to go to reconstruct such intimacy. Yet I believe this new/old paradigm not only holds a key to our future as a species, but can also inspire the next great renewal of a church that will squarely face the looming ecological endgame.

The vision of Watershed Discipleship as a framing theology and practice is resonating around North America, among ecumenically disparate communities including:

- Anglicans in Vancouver, B.C.[3],
- The Creation Care Network of the Mennonite Church USA,
- Presbyterians in Minnesota and North Carolina[4],
- African-American community organizers in the West Atlanta Watershed Alliance[5],
- Lutherans in Portland running the Ecofaith Recovery Project[6],
- and in my own watershed, the Ventura River Watershed Council is a shining example of community stakeholders coming together to do effective watershed planning[7].

Re-placed ecclesial communities can make an enormous contribution to the wider struggle to reverse social and ecological catastrophe – and in the process, recover the soul of our faith tradition.

[3] *See Rev. Laurel Dykstra's Ted-style talk at:*
http://ww2.anglican.ca/kat/video/watershed-discipleship/
[4] Minister activist Stuart Taylor has spearheaded a community-based "Watershed Now" campaign; see
https://www.youtube.com/watch?v=kYNI_8iWyzc
[5] *http://wawa-online.org/*
[6] *http://www.ecofaithrecovery.org/*
[7] *http://venturawatershed.org/*

We Christians are deeply culpable in the present crisis, but we also have ancient resources for the deep shifts needed. Watershed discipleship believes that only by "taking root downward," as the old prophet Isaiah put it, "can the surviving remnant...again bear fruit upward" (Isaiah 37:31)[8].

-CM

Inhabiting the Land
Rick Ufford-Chase

When I arrived in the Arizona borderlands in May of 1987, one of the first people I met was a Quaker philosopher and rancher by the name of Jim Corbett. Jim was unassuming in every way. He drove a beat-up Toyota and had to clear piles of debris from the front seat the first time that he picked me up. He was small of stature, and his fingers and toes were doubled back on themselves from a chronic condition of arthritis. He wore old jeans, a worn hat and a jean jacket, and he smelled of horses and cows and goats. He was, without a doubt, the smartest person I have ever met. He had an easy smile and a quiet manner that was endearing because it so clearly was not a put-on.

No one has shaped my thinking or my faith or my approach to organizing more than Jim Corbett. I arrived in the borderlands at just the right moment. Jim had just been tried in a federal court (though not convicted) for his work smuggling refugees who were fleeing the death squads and military dictatorships of Central America across the U.S./Mexico border to get them to safety. His

---

[8] For more information on this movement: *http://watersheddiscipleship.org/*; *www.facebook.com/groups/watersheddiscipleship/*. See also my longer exposition, "From 'Creation Care' to 'Watershed Discipleship': Re-Placing Ecological Theology and Practice," Conrad Grebel Review, Fall, 2014 (available at *https://uwaterloo.ca/grebel/publications/conrad-grebel-review/issues/fall-2014/creation-care-watershed-discipleship-re-placing-ecological*), and the forthcoming anthology Watershed Discipleship: Reinhabiting Bioregional Faith and Practice (Cascade Books, 2016).

life had been consumed by the Sanctuary movement for nearly a decade, and although he remained connected to that important human rights effort, his attention was beginning to shift back to a concern he believed was actually more important. Jim had his eye on the confluence of the Hot Springs Canyon and the San Pedro River, located about forty miles over the mountains to the east of Tucson in the Upper San Pedro watershed.

Jim and a group of friends had identified Hot Springs Canyon as a critically important corridor for east/west animal migratory flows. There is no other path allowing animals to survive the brutal desert ecosystem as they try to move between the Galiuro Mountains on the east side of the sixty-mile wide valley to the Rincon Mountains and the San Pedro River on the west. Although there was a nature preserve called the Muleshoe Ranch where the Hot Springs wash ran perennially, most of the native grasses in the lower part of the canyon were gone, and the wide wash was a favorite of outdoor sports enthusiasts who were destroying the ecosystem of the canyon with their four-wheel drive vehicles.

Jim's vision was elegant in its simplicity. If thirty or forty people could pool their financial resources, they might be able to purchase a 135-acre parcel at the mouth of the canyon, control access upstream, and begin to rebuild the riparian ecosystem upon which most of the desert wildlife depended. The project, called the Saguaro Juniper Corporation for its unique commitment to eschew a nonprofit approach to cooperative land management and for its equally unique elevation in the desert that allowed both the Saguaro cactus and Juniper Bushes to grow, is unlike any other land reclamation or conservation project I've ever seen. Jim was convinced that non-profit attempts to remove humans and livestock from protected areas were often misguided, and that instead there could be a symbiosis between human use and the ecology of the region that could serve the interests of both.

The first time that I agreed to meet Jim on the land, I used a map he had drawn on the back of a paper napkin from a Mexican restaurant where we had shared a meal. He drew it effortlessly, directing me to drive up ranch roads and across washes and gullies, following a left hand Y here, and a right hand fork in the canyon there, to meet him where he was tending his goats about four miles off the road that ran along the San Pedro River. I was accompanied by a group of seminarians from a school in the east who wanted to meet with Jim, and after nearly an hour of taking wrong turns, following canyon washes till they petered out, and then doubling back and trying again, we finally discovered Jim's forty-year-old pick-up tucked into a little sandy cul-de-sac under some juniper trees. Jim had strung a tarp from the back of the pickup to the ground and secured the bottom with rocks, and he invited the seven or eight of us to join him under the tarp and to share some of the warm milk he had just milked from his goats.

It was my first exposure to Jim's thinking, which was the basis for the Saguaro Juniper land covenant. Essentially, he proposed a Bill of Rights for the land that was designed to govern the human use of the property that the Saguaro Juniper Corporation was about to purchase[9]. The brilliance was at least three-fold. First, the covenant would allow Hot Springs Canyon to become a rich riparian ecosystem once again, thereby protecting a key component of the watershed. Second, if it worked, Jim believed that the value of the covenant would be so compelling that other landowners in the region would eventually begin to adopt the covenant on their properties as well, effectively extending a system of values of land governance far beyond the ability of any one individual to control the land. Finally, with a wisdom echoed in Ched's essay, Jim insisted that the best thing we could do for the environmental degradation taking place all around us was to root ourselves firmly in this valley and protect a specific ecosystem. I was hooked. I purchased a minimum share in the Saguaro Juniper corporation (something I could afford to do even on a volunteer stipend), and I spent many

---

[9] *http://www.saguaro-juniper.com/covenant/covenant.html*

hours on the land with Jim and other friends over the years to come.

One of the things I most appreciated about Jim's vision, which has now spawned many other projects and been a fundamental element in the repair of the ecosystem of the San Pedro River, is that it drew many of us from different theological traditions – and many from no theological tradition – into a common project that was actually quite theological in nature. This was, in many ways, a project of "being church" – a theological reorientation away from historic Christian understandings of the right and responsibility of humankind to have dominion over and subdue all other animals and all living things. Jim's notion of the symbiosis of our interactions with the land was essentially a spiritual one, though it worked itself out in very concrete ways.

Further, Jim simply refused to lend credence to the long-running feuds between environmentalists and ranchers that have characterized the western states for decades. He insisted that no one was in a better position than a rancher to care for the land, and that it could be done in a way that would actually prove to protect the ranchers' livelihoods, as opposed to forcing the ranchers off the land and protecting vast tracts of land through agencies like the Federal Bureau of Land Management. In the end, the wisdom and creativity of Jim's thinking are evident in the beauty and the rich biodiversity of Hot Springs Canyon thirty years after we purchased that original one hundred and thirty-five acres, and more than ten years after his death.

It should not surprise the reader that Ched Myers was a friend of Jim's and a student of his teaching. The work that Ched has been doing, built around his remarkable articulation of the watershed as the central way to define our communities, would have pleased Jim to no end. There is no more revolutionary possibility offered to the church in the United States today than the challenge that Ched puts before us.

Think about what watershed discipleship could mean to a small congregation that is dwindling in numbers and failing in vision. Imagine how it could affect a small group of friends who have little interest in traditional expressions of church but are deeply committed to constructing genuine, spiritually-grounded alternatives to the empty promises of the dominant culture. Envision a group of city dwellers who are seeking a way to reclaim and repair the urban ecosystems in their community. What if watershed discipleship was the first act of being church? What if, over the course of a generation, dozens or even hundreds of similar efforts were nurtured across the country? I think Ched gets it exactly right: given the overwhelming threat we face, no work should be more central to the act of reimagining the church than the work of repairing and renewing our local watersheds.

It is not so hard to imagine such a reawakening in our communities.

What would happen if our religious communities placed this commitment at the center of our lives together? Spend a little time in the company of Ched and his colleagues, and the impossible begins to look not just possible, but inevitable. We don't need to look far to find urban churches next to polluted watercourses or rural communities facing groundwater contamination from fracking or giant power projects that put our mighty rivers at risk. Our churches are in the heart of coastal communities that are endangered as sea levels rise and "One Hundred Year" storms recur with alarming frequency, and they are the heart and soul of the disaster response efforts that are becoming a regular and expected necessity. There's not a church in the country that doesn't depend on the watershed in which it is located for its very survival.

Unyoking ourselves and our communities from our dependency upon an anti-creation/anti-earth, extractionist economy has become an act of faith. Our churches must be re-imagined as the engines of resistance that will power our effort to advocate against the toxic, consumer economy that treats our environment as a commodity to be bought and sold for short-term gain.

> **Our churches must be re-imagined as the engines of resistance.**

No commitment will be more salient for those who live on the underside of the global economy or who exist outside the borders of the Empire. We know that climate change and the destruction of our environment will always fall hardest and fastest on those who don't have the resources to protect themselves or to move away from the crisis. As first world people of privilege (whatever part of the world we may live in), it is our ability to escape that actually puts all of us at risk. Ask the people of Flint if the decision to use non-treated, highly-corrosive drinking water would have been made if those in power would have had to give the water to their own children to drink or bathe in.

Over the last eight years, I have gathered most mornings to read a Psalm with a few members of my community. Slowly, I have become familiar with the poetry, and have developed favorites. Among those favorites is this passage from Psalm 65:

> *You visit the earth and water it,*
> *You greatly enrich it;*
> *The river of God is full of water;*
> *You provide the people with grain;*
> *For so you have prepared it.*
>
> *You water its furrows abundantly,*
> *Settling its ridges,*
> *Softening it with showers,*

And blessing its growth.

You crown the year with your bounty,
Your wagon tracks overflow with richness;
The pastures of the wilderness overflow,
The hills gird themselves with joy,
The meadows clothe themselves with flocks
The valleys deck themselves with grain
They shout and sing together for joy!

This is the Psalm that comes to mind when I think of what it might look like if our churches made watershed discipleship their first act. This vision seems so distant when I read of environmental destruction around the world and in my own backyard here in the Hudson Valley, and yet we are called to acts of great imagination that can be cultivated first in our faith communities. When we understand ourselves to be rooted in our watersheds – along with all the other living things in our ecosystem - the path toward greater faithfulness in our individual practices begins to seem more manageable.

This is where I return to the power of church, and some suggestions about ways to get started. As a member of a very small Presbyterian church, I am all too aware of the challenges confronting the few of us who are left. Our lives are busy and full. What little time we have left for the practice of being church seems to get sucked into maintaining our weekly worship service, acting as landlord to a variety of tenants who use our building, and assuring that the bills get paid.

The steps are simple, though not easy. This project will take intentionality and a willingness to let go of what feels urgent to us in order to focus on what is actually critically important.

- Together, we must embrace a shared vision for how we might begin to inhabit the watershed in which we reside.

- We'll need to pool our resources and redirect our energy to take action that would never be possible as individuals.

- Slowly, we will begin to sense that we are engaged in a sacred project, and our renewed spirit is likely to lead us to redefine exactly what we mean when we define our faith community.

- As our impact grows, and we connect with others making similar commitments in their own watersheds, the church actually has the potential to be a powerful force for good in the project of reclaiming and renewing.

This is what I know to be true. We act our way into right relationship with the earth. We become co-creators with God in the task of reclaiming and recovering God's gift of Creation. We commit.

-RUC

Discussion Questions:

1. Describe the ways in which you are already responding to the crisis of climate change.

2. What watershed are you located in? What do you know about the threats to the land in your region?

3. Visit the website for the Saguaro Juniper Corporation at http://www.saguaro-juniper.com and take the time to follow some of the links. What excites you as you read about the project? What ideas come up for you?

4. How could a commitment to fully inhabit the watershed in which you live transform your faith community? Where would you begin?

5. Rick finished the chapter with these words: *We act our way into right relationship with the earth. We become co-creators with God in the task of reclaiming and recovering God's gift of Creation. We commit.* What do his words make you think or feel?

Chapter 4
Learning Nonviolence in a Multifaith World

Mutual Dependence or Mutual Destruction
Rabia Terri Harris

I assume that we share a deep concern over our current situation: the huge planetary shift that manifests itself directly in climate change and indirectly in massive movements of human population, with all the passionate and violent struggles surrounding them. The experiential accompaniment of all this is an unprecedented disorientation, a loss of bearings on a global scale. Wherever we turn, an elemental sense of security – once taken for granted by nearly everybody – has now been replaced by a pervasive sense of longing, and of threat.

This moment in time requires a leap in our thinking, an historic change of attitude. Right now, I would argue, everything depends on abandoning the ego for the heart. And we must make that choice not just as individuals, but also as communities. It is time to lay down our arms.

In the Fatiha, the most fundamental of Muslim prayers, God is invoked as rabb ul-`alamin: Cherisher and Sustainer of all the worlds. What would happen if human beings were to actively embrace the vision that our identities, all of them – religious and otherwise – are cherished and sustained by God? What would happen if believers were to do so? How many would it take to reach a tipping point?

I write this as a conscious Muslim addressing those whom I hope are conscious Christians. I am painfully aware of the current conflicts among adherents of our traditions, and I will not minimize the differences in our theologies. I would like to suggest, however, that in this era, the common work we have to do is immeasurably more important than whatever tends to drive us apart. And in this era, if we do not take an explicit position on behalf of that common work, while grasping that our differences are indispensable to it, it seems to me that we are complicit in destruction.

Theological differences are human. Human images of God, or ultimate reality, develop out of the conversations of particular communities, address the needs of those communities, and are validated by the methods current in those communities. The object of each is to sanctify and justify the life of its community by connecting the daily business of living to the absolute mystery that surrounds us. This is how things have to work when finite beings turn to face the infinite. It's how we make sense of things, how we find meaning in what confounds us. What lens do we have to look through but ourselves? And what self exists apart from the complex web of relations that constructs the identity of each of us?

Yet if we only talk with people of our own religious community, we are very likely to be led astray...for a convergence of views tends to lead to the exclusion of facts.

The problem arises when we insist that our religion defines the holy, rather than humbly approximating it: that our image of ultimate reality is ultimate reality. Whenever people make such a claim, we set ourselves up as equal to reality itself. Such a situation is inherently unstable, since reality is obviously much bigger than we are, and cannot be made to go away. Yet until the inevitable reckoning occurs, it feels so very good to be in possession of the truth.

The grandiosity of the group tempts all communities. Buddhist teacher David Loy has brilliantly termed this phenomenon "wego" – or ego writ large. (The Prophet Muhammad called it `asabiyya.) Such heedless self-absorption is not less troublesome in communities than in single persons. It is more. It is the fundamental mechanism behind every war. It is the root cause of social injustice.

The phenomenon is natural. Nature bestows on every species a drive toward expansion that is part of a complex system of checks and balances. The human species, however, has managed to override these natural constraints. Consequently, we currently imperil not only ourselves but many other species through the blind pursuit of growth…that is, through instinct. The huge open question before us is whether we will find the means to override this natural instinct – to become self-constraining. Such a step would require transcending nature for the sake of nature: we would have to find a way to stop looking at the world around us "only personally."

What the human species has done as a whole, every human subcommunity is inclined to attempt as well. The dilemma of the whole is the dilemma of every part. Groups are driven to fulfill their instinct for growth, and that growth is routinely pursued at the expense of other groups. While we are expanding we feel successful, we feel right, we feel justified. We build whole theologies of self-justification! Our success convinces us that our image of ultimate reality is ultimate reality… and so one after another, successful groups fall into the same trap. We begin to worship ourselves, which is the real meaning of idolatry.

Idolatrous theologies are seductive because growth without constraint seems so much to a community's advantage. The universal prophetic argument, however, states that these theologies are wrong, and that what people take for glory is catastrophically to our disadvantage.

The last thing any successful group wants to hear is the annoying suggestion that our celebration of imminent triumph is ugly, and unnecessary, and false. Such a voice is rarely hard to come by, however – whether in the world of human beings or in the world of imagination, we will hear its accusations. It is the voice of the enemy. The voice of the enemy is the voice of illegal reality, of reality beyond our self-justifications. "That of God" which we have rejected speaks to us in the voice of the enemy. The voice of the enemy is often the prophetic voice.

If we do not wish to be counted among the rejecters of the prophets, then we must have the strength to see ourselves, not only as we would like to be seen, but also as our opposition sees us. We must grant them, humbly, what they are trying to say. Then opponents stop being enemies, and become teachers instead.

Of course this transformation will affect our self-importance! But actually nothing valuable is lost through such humility, while a very great deal is gained.

The Qur'an says:

> O human beings! Behold, we have created you all out of a male and a female, and have made you into nations and tribes, so that you might come to know one another. Verily the noblest of you in the sight of God is the one who is most deeply conscious of God. Behold, God is all-knowing, all-aware. (Hujurat 49:13)

"Coming to know" is a process. "The enemy" is a frozen concept. Resolving the problem before us requires us to look at the world in terms of processes, rather than frozen concepts – to keep our categories fluid, to break the identification of persons with the roles they play in particular situations. And it may be that when a sufficient number of people develop this skill, we will all find ourselves in a very different place.

Religions are often positioned as competitors, and competition is beneficial and adaptive under most circumstances. In the human, as in the natural world, evolution relies upon it. Yet at times, competition becomes diabolical. Sometimes the fear of losing becomes so intense that striving to outperform one's opponents is no longer enough: the possibility of opposition itself must be eliminated. For those afflicted with this fear, losing – losing face, losing ground – presents itself as equivalent to annihilation. To lose feels like ceasing to exist. Loss means shame, and shame to this degree is widely recognized as the most excruciating of emotions. We would often rather die than feel it. We would often rather kill. Obsession by this fear is one of the hallmarks of idolatry. It produces the need to destroy.

Perhaps the craving for total domination is a kind of spiritual virus: a sort of mutated objective, which, wherever it enters the natural process, moves the whole enterprise from a state of health to a state of sickness. I am suggesting that the desire for absolute supremacy may be the ultimate pathogen on the planet.

Perfectly good people, and perfectly good ideas, can be vectors of this virus, which travels invisibly, dormant in high ideals. Yet an outbreak is easy to diagnose. When my opponent refers to me in terms that are less than human, then my opponent has become symptomatic. When I refer to my opponent in terms that are less than human, then I have become symptomatic. And if either of us seeks to obliterate the other, then there are no two ways about it: it is the sickness acting, and we must be enormously careful that the contagion does not travel further.

The Qur'an says:

> The good deed and the evil deed are not alike. Repel evil with that which is better; then the one between whom and you was enmity will become like an intimate friend (Fussilat 41:34)

If we give up worshiping images of the Enemy, then their power over us will dissolve. A very different power will become evident in their place: "the creator of heaven and earth and of everything between them," in the Qur'anic phrase. What we call that power is up to us, but there are real advantages to calling it God. For once we do, we have access to the accumulated wisdom of the Abrahamic traditions: thousands of years of guidance. And we are no longer alone in the universe. Once we locate God as a living reality, rather than as a frozen concept – once we grasp the Cherisher and Sustainer of All the Worlds – it becomes much harder to take things "only personally" or to succumb to devastating fears. For both we and our opponent are embraced by the divine.

Suppose all it takes is an affirmation – a profound affirmation, a decision of the heart – that every knowledge is encompassed by mystery, and that I'm willing to live with that. Suppose that our self-knowledge is encompassed by mystery. Suppose that everything we encounter here belongs.

This is the position known in my tradition as tawhid, or affirming the unity. Nobody has to make the unity happen: it already exists. Accepting its existence has all kinds of implications for how we live, for how we might live. It's up to us whether we act on those implications or not.

God says, in an extra-Qur'anic prophetic report, or hadith qudsi, *When I created the creation, I inscribed upon the Throne, "My mercy overpowers My wrath."*

God is infinite. Yet since mercy and closeness are dearer to God than wrath and distance, God is always inviting us into a new intimacy. Can it be that we have all been catapulted into each other's presence because recognizing more of each other means recognizing more of God?

When we accept each other in God, we learn to recognize God through other names – names God has taught to people other than ourselves, to creatures other than ourselves. Might our time require that we learn to honor the immensity of the divine names?

It is the possibility of recognizing each other in God, I believe, that a new worldview (long in preparation) is now offering to human beings on a large scale for the first time. It provides, at the level of spirit, what ecology provides at the level of nature: a realization of belonging that calls us from our restless dreams of endless growth into the revelatory rhythms of dynamic balance.

It comes down to this: since we can no longer escape each other, if we are not to destroy each other, then we must ultimately acknowledge that we need each other. That discovery cannot occur too soon. You and I can assist this holy process. For in our time, there is a real chance of radically decreasing mutual disrespect...and that could make all the difference in the world.
-RTH

> ...if we are not to destroy each other, then we must ultimately acknowledge that we need each other.

Coming Down From Our Pedestal
Rick Ufford-Chase

Rabia and I live in a unique multifaith experiment called the Community of Living Traditions. Located at Stony Point Center in the Hudson Valley, our Abrahamic community of twenty Muslims, Jews and Christians dedicates itself to the work of offering hospitality and practicing nonviolence. Together, we commit to a radical proposition: it is a sacred project to learn one another's

> It is a sacred project to learn one another's rhythms and practices.

rhythms and practices and to understand and appreciate one another's core motivations and convictions – without attempting to change or convert one another in the process.

What makes this a meaningful experiment is not that it has never been done before (it has – on a far grander scale than ours), but that we are intentionally carrying it out in a moment in time marked by fear and hostility and acts of aggression committed by Christians, Jews and Muslims against one another. That violence places the entire world at risk.

What if, we posit, our three Abrahamic communities simply committed not to kill one another? As Rabia puts it in her essay, *"what would happen if human beings were actively to embrace the vision that our identities, all of them – religious and otherwise – are cherished and sustained by God?"*

Shortly after the attacks of 9/11/2001, John Paul Lederach penned his "Traveling Essay"[1] in which he presciently named the challenge before our nation – to destroy the myth that each side seeks to sustain as justification for their actions. That myth – of a battle between good and evil, or between faithful and apostate, drives the actions of both sides. For the west, it justifies constant, overwhelming use of military force that makes it ever easier for the "terrorists" to sell their myth and entice more and more recruits to sacrifice their lives in terrorist bombings that seem inexplicable to the rest of the world. This in turn justifies even greater military aggression from so-called "civilized" nations that is sustained through an ever-growing and carefully cultivated fear of the other. This, Lederach warned, would be a never-ending cycle of violence.

---

[1] http://www.mediate.com/articles/terror911.cfm

Unfortunately, he appears to have been exactly right in his prediction.

The Community of Living Traditions was born as a direct response to this cycle of violence. We insist that our first act must be to build deep relationships based on mutual understanding of one another, appreciation of our differences, and commitment to seek common ground. We stand against those in each of our traditions who corrupt our sacred text to justify acts of violence against one another. We honor what Rabia has suggested is a unique, historic opportunity to renounce the tendency in each of our traditions to seek endless growth and evolve instead toward the "revelatory rhythms of dynamic balance."

I love the Qur'anic verse that Rabia lifts up in this context, for it echoes my own favorite teaching of Jesus. It is striking to read them together:

> The good deed and the evil deed are not alike. Repel evil with that which is better; then the one between whom and you was enmity will become like an intimate friend (Fussilat 41:34)

And...

> But I say to you that listen, Love your enemies, do good to those who hurt you, bless those who curse you, pray for those who abuse you. (Luke 6:27 and 28)

I propose that this text should be among a handful of most important scriptures to ground the Christian church of the next generation. What would it look like for Christians to take responsibility to model an entirely different way of responding to the threat we perceive?

After seven years of living in the Community of Living Traditions, I am coming to terms with the reality that, for most of us, we must begin by admitting our unrecognized privilege. For me, this has felt much like similar work I have had to do to come to terms with the unearned privilege associated with being male, straight, white, and a U.S. citizen. Early in our work together as a community, my Jewish and Muslim colleagues began to hold me accountable for the ways Christian privilege in the United States shapes me: a position we are slowly losing as the changing demographic reality of the U.S. population takes hold, forcing us to actually own the values of freedom of religion which our country's founders enshrined in our Constitution.

This privilege shapes me, and all of us who are Christian, in ways that most of us who enjoy those privilege are not aware of, but that are obvious to those of other religious traditions. Our religious holidays are woven into the fabric of our national culture, our leisure, and even our work. Our churches are accustomed to being the primary architects of our nation's moral conscience. Worse, we assume that other religious traditions have nothing to offer in that endeavor. We make little or no effort to understand the most rudimentary elements of the significant religious celebrations in other traditions, like Rosh Hashanah and Yom Kippur in the lives of Jews, or Ramadan and Eid for Muslims. We routinely offer Christian prayers before public events but become uncomfortable and even suspicious at public expressions of piety or faithfulness by those who espouse something other than a faith in Jesus Christ.

Anyone who cares to seek can find these signs, but it is more challenging to name the invisible ways in which assumption of privilege marks our relationships with those who are not Christian. Gently, but firmly, members of the Community of Living Traditions have held the Christians in our community to account for the unexamined ways in which we set the agenda or establish our cultural mores.

For instance, early on, we worked to create safe, visible places where Muslims and Jews could feel welcome at Stony Point Center.

However, as our relationships have deepened it has become increasingly obvious that doing so actually creates an assumption that the entire campus is "Christian" and that Muslims and Jews are honored guests on what remains, essentially, Christian territory. The task is far greater than making Jews and Muslims feel welcome, it is to make our entire campus feel as if we are co-creators of a space that is "owned" by all of us. The next step, we realized, must be to create a particular space for Christians to feel comfortable, just as we have for those of other traditions, subtly insisting in the process that the larger campus is not "Christian," but instead a space where we must work together to assure that all people can feel welcome and at home.

This is a concrete example of what Rabia refers to early in her contribution when she writes of the need to address our desire to define God, which eventually leads to the idolatrous assumption of religious superiority. Rabia elevates this challenge, and the importance of our experiment as a community, in a way that I find deeply inspiring, when she proposes that taking an explicit position for the common work we must do together is critically important, even while it depends on grasping the reality of what differentiates us.

For hundreds of years Christians have taken the lead in articulating the fundamentals of the system of governance in the United States. I was raised on stories about how the Presbyterian polity helped to shape the U.S. Constitution, and it was a source of some pride for First Presbyterian Church in York that a signer of the Declaration of Independence was buried in our cemetery. Protestant Churches are physically located right in the center of most towns and cities across the country, and we have long-expected that our experience was the foundation of the moral conscience in most of our communities. Our members have traditionally been people with economic, social and political power, sitting on the boards both of for-profit corporations and nonprofit organizations, and offering leadership at all levels of government. Even as recently as forty years ago, my own elementary school offered Christian prayer to begin each day, and the practice remains prevalent at sports events and academic convocations across the country. There is not a problem with invoking God in the midst of our public life; it's that our hidden assumption is that we mean the Christian God. Other understandings of God actually make many of us quite uncomfortable, especially when referenced in any kind of public way.

However, our communities have changed dramatically in the last generation. Significant numbers of adherents of non-Christian traditions reside even in small towns across the country. Combine this with the secularization of our culture in which many people do not overtly identify with any religious tradition, and we suddenly find that a fairly small minority of our citizens sit in a Christian church on a typical Sunday morning. This shift is unmistakable where I live in the northeast, and our region is a bellwether for the changes that later impact cities and towns across the United States.

In the far more religiously pluralistic communities of the next generation, to survive and to offer something creative and meaningful, Christians will have to articulate what we have to survive, and to embody something that will help to strengthen our society. We do this not because it is our right as the dominant religion, but because we have something compelling to share that helps to tear down walls of division and strengthens all of us in our religiously pluralistic communities.

Before going to live in a multifaith community, I heard people talk about how being in a healthy interfaith relationship made them a stronger Christian. I think I would say the same after seven years in the Community of Living Traditions, but I confess that my path to get there has been rocky, and it has everything to do with the too-easy sense of entitlement I carried as a Christian when our experiment began.

Early in our time together, I actually felt at risk. I think that was largely because the Muslim and Jewish members of our community were accustomed to a practice of ritual and prayer and observance of religious holidays that made me feel insecure and inadequate. This should have been no surprise, because these are all the things that minority cultures and religious traditions have always had to do to maintain a sense of their own identity in a culture that is fundamentally hostile to them. The flip side is that those who are part of the dominant culture often become lazy or complacent because we find little need to distinguish ourselves from the dominant culture. Over time, I have been pushed to examine and establish my own practices in a way that really has grounded me in my own tradition.

Many Christians, Presbyterians among them, have a practice of identifying and confessing our corporate sin. In my church, we do this every week, reading a shared confession that examines the ways we are complicit with structures and practices of injustice and the reality of broken relationships in the world. In spite of our unexamined privilege, we are actually well practiced at examining our assumptions of superiority as we embrace our role among a far more nuanced, rich and complex tapestry of religious identities. Our task is to move beyond tolerance and even beyond expressions of solidarity to build deeper relationships that set us up to let go of our own privilege, creating something new and entirely different with partners in other religious traditions who are similarly committed.

Gracefully letting go of our assumption of superiority may be the most important gift we have to offer to the project of building a multireligious voice for peace and ecological and social justice in a nation that is struggling to find its moral center. It is that vacuum that exists in our national psyche that makes the work of building authentic, multi-faith communities so exciting at this particular moment. While the enthusiasm for the institutional trappings of church has never been lower in our country than it is right now, the desire to connect with a spiritual grounding that counters the empty promises of the dominant culture is unmistakably on the rise.

Even as I write these words, I can hear the naysayers in my own tradition who are convinced I am endangering us all as I give up on the exclusive claim that Jesus is the only way to salvation. But Presbyterians, at least, and many others in the Christian traditions as well, have long since clarified our own position. In 2014, the Presbyterian Church (USA) affirmed an "Interreligious Stance" to provide a blueprint for building healthy relationships with partners of other traditions. It begins with this affirmation, which those in other Christian traditions may find helpful as well:

> The Presbyterian Church (U.S.A.) long has advocated positive relationships with people of other religious traditions. We have seen these relationships as a specific instance of Christ's universal command to "... love the Lord your God with all your heart, and with all your soul, and with all your mind" and to "love your neighbor as yourself" (Mt. 22:37, 39). This statement affirms that tradition.

We must insist that we are less safe, not more safe, when we assume that we have the right and responsibility to impose our religious, cultural, economic and political hegemony on others. This deeply-integrated part of our psyche as a nation provides the moral justification for Empire-building that we take for granted, just as members of Empire have done throughout history. As Rabia has suggested, this largely unrecognized conviction lies just below the surface in justifying a great deal of the violence in the world today. Christians do not have a corner on this market, as Rabia so clearly evidences in her contribution. Wouldn't it be amazing for Christians to model a sense of humility that could help all of us into a different way of being in relationship with one another?

For any Christian who feels weary of being told that the only response to the threat of a Quaddafi, or Hussein, or Al Qaeda, or

ISIS/ISIL (or whatever the latest evil is that must be abolished) is to lash out militarily to vanquish the enemy, the Presbyterian's "Interreligious Stance" is worth careful study and deliberation. It offers theological justification and guidance for those excited by the ways in which greater religious diversity strengthens our communities. The Interreligious Stance of the PC(USA) is one example of how Christians may examine what role God has in store for us in this new, complex web of relationships that redefine our fundamental assumptions of what it means to be followers of Jesus in the United States today.

As Christians, we can live our lives with passion and conviction and invite others to experience the Good News of the Gospel without assuming that we must be "more right" than everyone else. Our ability to thrive will not be secured through an act of force or military aggression. In the world of the 21st Century, no religious tradition will be able to assume a position of superiority – regardless how benevolent its intent.

We will find the security that we seek, which appears as natural instinct throughout human history, only when we can affirm what makes us most authentically who God calls us to be. What do we bring to the table that has the potential not just to keep us grounded as Christians, but also to enrich others who believe differently than we do? Are we capable of distinguishing ourselves from the empty promises of consumerism, selfishness and greed of the dominant culture in order to offer a genuine alternative to those who are seeking meaning over glitz and glitter?

The good news is that this is what Jesus was all about. In the final story from Matthew 25, Jesus tells his disciples just what we will be held accountable for on the day of judgment. Have we befriended and fed those who are hungry or thirsty? Did we welcome the immigrant - the stranger in our land? Did we offer shelter and clothing to those who were in need? Did we care for the sick in our community, and did we visit and advocate for the prisoner?

These are values I'm willing to be held accountable for. They offer a clear alternative to meaningless glitter promised by the Empire. If we who are followers of Jesus are willing to put this on the table as the hallmark for what it means to be Christian, I expect that we will find a great deal of common ground and a shared sense of purpose with sisters and brothers from other traditions, or from no religious tradition at all, who share these values.

-RUC

Discussion Questions:

1. What positive experiences have you had in building relationships with people of other faith traditions? Negative ones?

2. Rick cited the "Interreligious Stance" of the Presbyterian Church (USA), which can be found here - http://www.presbyterianmission.org/site_media/media/uploads/theologyandworship/interfaith/the_interreligious_stance_pc(usa)1.pdf
How is this document helpful regarding your own understanding about how to be in relationship with those who are not Christian?

3. Rabia writes *"Suppose all it takes is an affirmation – a profound affirmation, a decision of the heart – that every knowledge is encompassed by mystery, and that I'm willing to live with that. Suppose that our self-knowledge is encompassed by mystery. Suppose that everything we encounter here belongs."* Where does her musing take you?

4. Rick offers a strong critique of the ways in which Christianity has been watered down because of its dominance in the United States. He also shares the ways in which he has been challenged to examine his faith more deeply because of his close association with Jews and Muslims. How do you respond to his critique and his confession?

Chapter 5
Resisting the Seduction of Silence

Welcome Is More Than A Statement
Alex Patchin McNeill

For those who have experienced the church as a loving, warm community of believers faithfully following the call of Jesus, it can be hard to imagine what it must be like for someone to be afraid to walk through our doors out of fear of rejection.

Growing up, church was where I could be most myself. I learned to love Jesus while running around the fellowship hall after worship, clanging the handbells in the youth choir, and planning for the youth Sunday worship service. Before I had words to name the dissonance between my body, the gender I was expected to be, and who I felt I was on the inside, the church was the place that didn't ask me to explain myself, but loved me for who I was. I learned about God's unconditional love from the faith community that nurtured and accepted me as I first came out as a lesbian and later as a transgender man. My sense of call to the ministry was first and foremost a call to extend the feeling that church could be a place that felt like home to everyone.

After I finished seminary, my church attendance came to a screeching halt. I had moved to a new town as I was wrestling with my gender identity. I hadn't yet come out as transgender and most of the world still saw me as a woman. I had a man's short haircut and felt most comfortable in men's neckties and button-down shirts, but my soprano singing voice clearly marked me as someone born female. I stopped attending church because I was sick of the stares that followed me when I walked in to take a seat in a pew at the churches in my new town. I was tired of going to the fellowship hall after worship for coffee hour and not having anyone talk to me because I looked different than most of the church members. Though the sign outside of the church might read "all are welcome," I started feeling like a stranger in the one place I once felt the most at home.

Even though I never heard any negative statements against Lesbian, Gay, Bisexual and Transgender (LGBT) people from the pastor or congregation where I grew up, I suddenly became afraid to go to church. The true inclusiveness of my home church couldn't inoculate me against the microaggressions of other churches - those small, largely unnoticed, and often culturally-ingrained, habits that make it clear some people are not welcome there. It was devastating to feel as if I couldn't turn to the church during one of the most difficult times of my life. While no one said anything overtly negative about my gender-ambiguous appearance, the body-language of my fellow worshippers was enough to send the message that I made them uncomfortable. What became clear to me is that most of the churches I visited didn't have the language with which to welcome me as a transgender person in their midst, no matter their good intentions or declarations of "all are welcome".

In my first few years as Executive Director of More Light Presbyterians, an organization dedicated to the full inclusion of LGBT people in the Presbyterian Church (USA), I've had the chance to dream about what a truly inclusive church can be. I have seen the transformative power a deep posture of welcome can have on faith communities. I hope for this truly welcoming church to be a reality not just because of my role with More Light, but because I long to attend it myself. I yearn for fellowship for others whom I know feel isolated and alienated and exhausted by the awkward body language and smiles that don't reach people's eyes. The lesson I've learned is this:

welcome is more than a statement, and adopting a posture of welcome is an ongoing journey rather than an item to check off a list.

For some churches, becoming a welcoming church begins and ends with a formal statement of declaration about whom they will welcome in the faith community. While it is really important to name specifically those who have been marginalized in our society, simply listing those who are welcome does not mean that feeling of welcome will permeate through the whole community and into the hearts of those who fear rejection.

The churches that have truly been transformed into welcoming communities are all guided by the same principle: welcome is an ongoing process. The key is continuing to educate ourselves about who might be missing from God's table, and how we might extend welcome to those who haven't experienced it. Many of our foundational More Light churches started their journeys by learning about how to welcome gay people into their midst, but hadn't yet begun conversations about bisexual and transgender inclusion. For these churches, the welcoming journey continued by educating the congregation to better understand the perspective of bisexual and transgender folks so that they might be able to welcome them within the faith community.

> **This deep posture of welcome learned by these churches for LGBT people isn't the end of their journeys.**

The most welcoming churches are always in a state of learning, never complacent about having "done enough" or "checking off" the "welcome box." This deep posture of welcome learned by these churches for LGBT people isn't the end of their journeys. Once congregations learn how to see some who have been considered strangers, that new lens helps them to also see others who have not been welcomed traditionally.

One of our barriers in engaging this work is thinking that we are not enough, that the problem of exclusion is so much bigger than we are. However, the journey toward a transformative experience of welcome often begins with one person asking the question, "What else can my congregation do to welcome the stranger?" The truth is, others in your congregation may wonder the same thing. They may even have brothers, sisters, children or aunts they are hoping would feel welcome, too. The power of a truly inclusive congregation is that everyone feels fully seen and recognized as a child of God. This is the greatest gift of grace that we have the power to give. My dream is that every church be as inclusive as God's love.

-APM

The Courage of Our Convictions
Rick Ufford-Chase

I think what makes Alex's description of his experience of trying to feel included in a Presbyterian Church so moving is that his description of growing up in the church is so similar to my own, yet that of trying to find a place where he is genuinely welcome in the church as an adult is so divergent from my own. The question of whether and how to include people whose sexual orientation or gender identity is outside the normative cis-gender, heterosexual experience has plagued the Presbyterian Church (USA) for decades, and we are not alone.

I have chosen to use LGBTQ as the descriptor for people who share Alex's experience. Some are still participating in the traditional church, some have left for churches that have long-been more affirming of who they are, and a great many have abandoned the church or never thought of looking to the church because of the failure of our church institutions to welcome them. LGBT is meant to include Lesbians, Gay Men, Bisexuals, and Transgender People. Some people choose to include the letter "Q" to refer to all people who are Queer, and to include those who are gender non-conforming. This is meant to intentionally include those who identify as "Intersex" – meaning that they have physical characteristics that are not categorized as male or female, and those who are asexual – referring to persons who are not attracted to anyone or who don't have overt sexual orientations. "Q" can also be expanded to include those questioning sexual or gender identity and trying to figure things out. The remarkable thing, in my experience, is how making room for this kind of questioning opens us all to a significant community of people who have received a clear message that the Church has no interest in them.

After nearly forty years of struggle about whether and how to include the LGBTQ community in the life of the church, the Presbyterian Church (USA) has made changes to our constitution in the last few years that make it clear that we will be a fully welcoming and inclusive church. Being Lesbian or Gay or Transgender or Bisexual or Queer is not, in and of itself, an impediment to being ordained into leadership, nor is there, any longer, a prohibition against same-sex marriages.

We now confront a defining moment as a denomination that is potentially instructive for those in other religious traditions who are grappling with similar issues. Many in our community maintain their absolute conviction that our sacred text is clear that gender nonconformity is a sin. For many of them, the purity of the church is our highest aspiration and the lack of it our greatest potential downfall as a denomination. Many of our members, and even entire congregations, have chosen to leave the Presbyterian Church (USA) to its own fallenness and to seek another home. Others, equally concerned that our decision to allow for the full inclusion of those in the LGBTQ community represents a watering down of the gospel, have chosen to stay in the church that they love and to struggle to maintain what they see as a faithful witness to scriptural purity. Though I disagree with this theological analysis, I actually have a great deal of respect for the effort to assure that one's greatest values are reflected in one's institution. In fact, I share similar motivation in making the case for my own theological position.

I have far greater trouble with those who espouse a middle-of-the-road theology and moderation as our highest value. I believe this unfortunately describes the majority of those who call themselves Presbyterian – and maybe even the majority of Christians in the country – today. For them, the answer to the "where do we go from here" question is fairly straightforward: Don't make a big deal out of it. It's ok that we made this decision, but let's not announce it too loudly, nor go out of our way to repeat the affirmation within our services of worship. "After all," this line of reasoning goes, "we need to use care not to offend those who disagreed with our decision."

While I feel empathy for those whose viewpoint is no longer the official position of the church (after all, I have been in that position many times myself), and I am convinced of the need for graciousness, I believe there is no future in downplaying the significance of our action. Being bold (while gracious) in our proclamation and continuing path toward a fully-inclusive church are key elements in remaking our church. The conversation is far more broad than being inclusive of the LGBTQ community. This is a conversation about the kind of church we will be and the hallmarks that will define our faith communities for the next generation. It goes to the heart of the pathos that we are experiencing as Christians in the United States today.

We've named the threats represented by Empire, systems of white supremacy, climate change and our dislocation from the land that sustains us, and religious superiority and the violence it breeds. The final threat I want to name is the fear of our own demise as church.

All of the other threats we've named are from forces outside the church. These are the challenges faced by the entire world where the community of followers "on the way" of Jesus could make a real impact if we choose to fully embrace the gospel vision. The greatest threat to our soul as a body of believers is not from without, however – it is from within.

We fear that we are no longer relevant, that no one cares what we think, including many of the people who sit in our sanctuaries. We fear as our numbers dwindle that there is nothing to be done about it. We fear there is no one left to honor and care for our elders, and that our children and grandchildren will never be interested in the church. We fear that we will be unable to pay the bills and that the great edifices left to us by previous generations will crumble around us. We fear that we will not be able to afford a full-time pastor, and we can't imagine what it means to be church without one. Though few of our churches have the courage to entertain an honest conversation about it, we fear our own extinction.

The people who have made a career out of supporting and shaping the institution of the church are the primary audience for this book. So let me say to you - I love you, and I care about the ways you try to provide pastoral leadership to a church that is desperate for a makeover. I have centered my vocation around the task of keeping one foot in the world of the church in which I grew up – a church of all kinds of privilege I have reflected on in these chapters. I am placing the other foot in the worlds where everyone else resides: those who are undocumented or LGBTQ or on the underside of the global economy, or those who are do not experience the system of white supremacy as a privilege but instead as oppression. I have built my entire ministry around my commitment to bring my people – white, straight people carrying all kinds of privilege – to an awakening about the true cost of following Jesus.

So I ask people like me who have given their lives to the church, can we admit that this thing we love is broken? Can we confess our fear as we watch our membership decline and budgets shrink? Can we open ourselves to the possibility that God may be working a new thing in our midst? This may be not a sign of the demise of everything we cherish, but instead an unbelievable opportunity to participate in the transformation and renewal of the spiritual life of the institution that has become the church.

If we can agree these are the fundamental questions, then the challenge is to diagnose what is wrong. Plenty of people across our church tell us the problem is that we have abandoned our principles on the questions of personal piety that grounded us for several generations. Depending on just how far they follow their own logic, they say the problem is that we have become far too permissive in our understanding of who is "in" and what behavior is acceptable. Their voices are often subtle, but still remarkably clear: "LGBTQ folks are good people but their behavior is sinful." "Divorced people are fallen." "Women are not suited to leadership." "Black Lives Don't Matter." "Native and Indigenous Peoples don't exist anymore, and their spirituality is a threat." The list is actually quite long, and figuring out where to stop once we've started down the road to defining who is "in" and who is "out" is next to impossible.

The biggest problem I have with these attitudes is that Jesus didn't share them. Many of Jesus' contemporaries were concerned that too many problematic populations were being let in. Far from echoing that concern, Jesus' own questions revolved around how to include those who engendered the most fear in his religious community. He ate with sinners and challenged the purity laws and spent time among the Gentiles and refused to condemn sex workers. His preoccupation was with those who should be included, not those who should be excluded. If I must choose between traditional, often prejudicial understandings of whom God invites to the table and a wildly expansive invitation that continually challenges all of us to re-examine our prejudice, I'll take the latter.

Some people are less rigid in thinking that personal piety is the problem in our church. They are, however, convinced that the demise of our beloved institution is attributable to our uncomfortable habit of addressing controversial topics in our sacred spaces. In this analysis, politeness trumps everything. "I have plenty of conflict in my life every week without coming to church to find it here as well." Our preachers are expected to push us to be better people, preferably using good humor and folksy stories to make their points, but they are to stay far away from the political or social issues that divide us.

Here again, I can sympathize with the impulse, especially given how politically divided our country is at this point, but I can find no biblical justification for such a stance. I'm trying to think of a time when Jesus taught his followers to stay out of the fray, and it's hard to come up with it. On the contrary, he called out the Roman military, refused to cower before Pontius Pilate, challenged his own religious leaders for their narrowness, turned common notions of fair wage upside down, consistently called out those who attempted to get ahead at the expense of their neighbors, and repeatedly asked his followers to care for the throwaways for whom the rest of their society had no use.

So once again, if forced to choose between being a "good moderate" or risking everything to promote a vision genuinely rooted in the Gospel – I'll take door number two.

The mainline Christian church of the last century was able to define itself primarily based on the number of adherents it claimed and the influence it wielded in the dominant culture and political realm. There is no way that either membership or political or pop culture dominance will define the mainline church in the United States in the 21st Century. We exist in a world that is largely secular, and in which there are exponentially more religious and spiritual choices available to us than in the past. Our task, in our time and our particular context, is to name the distinctive commitments we bring to the table and to own those commitments boldly and authentically.

Our goal should be clear: welcome anyone who desires to be a genuine disciple of the radical Jesus. Whom we invite in should be defined not by who seems most acceptable or most moral, but instead by who appears to be committed to re-orienting their lives to gospel values and a gospel vision.

As for the kind of community I want to be a part of, I am interested in creating a community where those who have been rejected in every other space can come and feel safe. I am seeking people who believe in confession and personal testimony about the things they are really struggling with in their lives. I am looking for allies who are willing to say "no" to facile platitudes that lead us into war over and over again, or who firmly support and take action in the Black Lives Matter movement, or who want to take on climate change or gun violence or the fight for a fifteen-dollar minimum wage because they know that these are biblical questions. In essence, I am interested in people with an evangelical spirit who are unwavering in their commitment to social justice, and who recognize their own complicity in the structures of domination and oppression in which we all participate. This is what church should look like.

The Presbyterian Church, along with many of our sister mainline denominations, has a lot to be proud of. Though it has often taken far too long for us to get there, we are solid in our conviction that sexism has no place in our church and that women are welcome in all aspects of leadership. Many of our churches and pastors took genuine risks during the civil rights movement of the sixties. We have taken a clear position against gun violence. We have made our welcome to immigrants quite clear. We were early in our condemnation of the War in Iraq. We have confessed our complicity for the holocaust and spent the last sixty years working to atone for it, insisting that we will condemn Anti-Semitism and refuse to allow our sacred text to provide the justification for continued anti-Jewish bigotry. We are among the first to show up when Islamophobia or racism manifest themselves in our communities. We have striven repeatedly and over many decades to assure that our financial investments match our social witness policy. And now, finally, we have come down on the side of full-inclusion of the LGBTQ community.

Let's not soft-pedal our gospel-grounded vision of a church that welcomes all people who are doing their best to give everything over to God and to follow the way of the cross. This is a time to be clear. If you are Gay or Lesbian or Bisexual or Transgender or still trying to figure out your own sexual or gender identity, we see beauty in who God has created you to be, and in all the other things that you are beyond gender and sexual identity: you are welcome with us. If you have been wounded by your experience of church and you are looking for a home where your gifts will be honored and you will be supported in your struggles, we want you to be a part of our community. If you are struggling with broken relationships, or seeking to lead a life of meaning, we are with you.

> Let's be for something, and let that something be not exclusion, but inclusion.

Let's be for something, and let that something be not exclusion, but inclusion. Let's not apologize for the courageous campaigns we undertake for justice, but instead own them without fear. Our country is in desperate need of communities of tolerance. With each passing day it seems that we in the United States grow more intolerant of one another. Let's create a church that offers an alternative - that presents hope and welcome and the full-gospel vision of Jesus Christ to all who are curious enough to enter.

Alex McNeill, whose wisdom opened this chapter, offers some wonderful examples of how faith communities can strive to become truly inclusive spaces:

- Make welcome visible. How might your faith community visually represent its welcome? For those who have been shut out of faith communities, a visual sign that they are included is a powerful way to help people trust that your community sees them for all of who they are. In some LGBT affirming churches, the visible sign of welcome has included a rainbow flag or sticker a visitor could spot before one enters the building. How is welcome visible out in your community? Where are some opportunities to help your church's support be known? Whether it is marching in the LGBT Pride Parade in your town or hosting an event at an LGBT-run business, for those who have been hurt by their churches, a welcoming congregation out in the community will go a long way to build the trust that your church is a safe space.

- Understand the power of words: If your congregation has written a welcoming statement, in what ways does it become a living document? Is it read at the beginning of each worship service? If you are a welcoming community, how often are themes of welcome included in worship liturgies or the sermon? It is truly mind boggling how many people have experienced church-based trauma for some part of their identity – a word of welcome can be an incredibly healing part of worship.

- Extend welcome into leadership: Is your faith community nurturing a diverse group of leaders within the congregation and supporting their full participation in the life of the community? For those who have been shut out of the church, actively seeking to find ways to incorporate their voice in worship leadership, or their gifts in ministry to the church, both broadens the horizon of the community and fosters a deep sense of connection and inclusion. For LGBT people and other marginalized voices, seeing ourselves reflected in the church's leadership is a powerful indication of welcome.

- Using your church's space to offer welcome: One of the greatest resources we have as churches is the use of the building itself to be a welcoming place to those attending worship and as a tool for ministry beyond Sunday services. What are some of the ways your church space could help extend welcome? For example, some churches have sought to further welcome transgender people by dedicating a single stall bathroom as a gender-neutral restroom. Other churches have partnered with LGBT-affirming community groups to offer space for meetings during the week. Our church buildings can be a wonderful way to evangelize the welcoming nature of the congregation.

To make visible the kind of welcome that Alex proposes is to embark on a journey whose final destination cannot be known. Each time I take a risk and genuinely open myself to someone who has been excluded in the dominant socio-economic paradigm, I find myself entering into a new world that I otherwise never would have experienced. I think this is the heart of the invitation Jesus extended in the fourth chapter of Matthew when he asked James and John and Andrew and Simon Peter to put down their nets and follow him. There is no final destination for those of us who seek to be followers of Jesus, and I am suspicious of anyone who claims ultimate knowledge of what our arrival in the promised land might look like. Faith is the act of embracing the unknown.

-RUC

Discussion Questions:

1.   Have you ever had an experience similar to Alex's, sensing that you are not welcome? Describe your experience.

2.   What do you think of this statement of Rick's? "As for the kind of community I want to be a part of, I am interested in creating a community where those who have been rejected in every other space can come and feel safe." If you had to name what you value most highly in a community, what would be at the top of the list?

3.   What do you think of Alex's list, at the end of the chapter, on how communities can become truly inclusive places of welcome? If you were to make your own list as a community, what would be on it?

4.   Read Matthew 4:12-25. Note the death of John the Baptist, Jesus' choosing to begin his ministry with a call to repent, and the call stories of the fisherman. What do you think about Rick's use of this story to highlight the nature of what it means to be embrace the unknown?

Part Two
Gospel Visions

Chapter 6
The Local Congregation as the Locus of Resistance

What is Worship?
Brian Merritt and Mercy Junction

As we stood out in the cold, the members of Mercy Junction felt invigorated.

On our Bible study night, we walked a picket line. Announcing this action as "Praying with Our Feet," friends of Mercy Junction joined a group of men whose human rights had been violated by their boss. Each step I took connected me to something greater than myself – solidarity with the earth that grounds us to each other through gravity, solidarity with activists whose passion for justice mirrored the divine's, and solidarity with those who suffered oppression from Capitalism's cruel dehumanization in the workplace. As I walked the picket line, I imagined the divine, defiantly proud, her fist in the air, chanting along with us as we yelled for equality.

In these moments of action, my faith deepens. I feel free and full of the abundant life that Christ promised. I truly know we are living out Mercy Junction's hope for our community: "Gospel in practice with hands and feet, from the pews to the streets."

What is worship? We find ourselves asking this question at Mercy Junction Justice and Peace Center often. This came to a head when key decision-makers in the national Presbyterian church questioned our commitment to worship. We found ourselves confused and angry. Wasn't everything that we were doing a part of our faith and response to God? How did our denomination get such an incredibly small definition of worship? Was our own definition too big?

From our inception, we believed that every action we took publicly as a community was attached to our faith. As a Presbyterian Community, we began our discernment around the "Great Ends of the Church" outlined in our constitution, believing that our calling was to live out faith by proclaiming social righteousness to our community. We have a deep and abiding love of Scripture and its clear call for justice. Still, as we walk with workers in picket lines, we are challenged in our practice of the faith. Does following this sometimes radical path constitute worship?

Our heroes of the faith are people like Sarah Cleghorne (Quaker and animal rights activist), Jane Addams (Socialist founder of the Hull House and modern social worker movement), Toyohiko Kagawa (Japanese spiritual leader who worked in the slums of Tokyo), Dorothy Day (Christian Anarchist who helped found the Catholic Worker), Martin Luther King, Jr. (Civil Rights leader and Baptist Minister), Francis Grimke (Presbyterian Pastor and founder of the NAACP), Emily Pankhurst (British Suffragette), Mahatma Gandhi (Human rights champion and proponent of nonviolent resistance), Albert Schweitzer (Lutheran Medical Missionary to Africa and proponent of a Reverence for Life), Milton Galamison (Presbyterian Minister and agitator for the desegregation of the New York City Public School System) and Maggie Kuhn (Presbyterian lay leader and founder of the Grey Panthers working for the rights of elders).

There is truly nothing new under the sun. We know that in times past the Presbyterian Church has accepted radical notions of new worship. Charles Stelzle, eminent lay minister from the beginning of the 20th Century, made that apparent. Not only did Charles Stelzle head the Workingmen's Department of the Board of Home Missions of the Presbyterian Church (USA), work as a regular syndicated columnist to over 100 labor newspapers, and become a founder of Interfaith Worker Justice, but he also acted as the creative force behind the Labor Temple movement that dotted the landscape in the early 20th century. In New York City, Charles Stelzle claimed the Labor Temple to be "entirely unsectarian, where every man, if he have a message, may give it expression, and if it be good it will receive attention." On its opening day, Labor Temple was attended by five hundred labor union members, Socialists, Anarchists, sociologists, and other people who took interest in labor matters.

Mercy Junction Justice and Peace Center hopes to reclaim this history – a radical history too often suppressed by both moderate liberals and moderate conservatives to protect the institution. We hope to create a nonsectarian gathering space for the spiritual, the activist and the artist, a place where our spiritual practices as a gathered community lead to the direct action associated with worship.

So, what is worship? Through Mercy Junction's experience, study, reflection, and prayer, we believe there can be no distinction between the gathering and the active sending of the faithful out for mission in the world. This has clear practical theological implications for our community because it points to practical, actionable trajectories that each act of faith gives to us as followers of Jesus Christ, like hospitality, reflection, and radical acts of salvific defiance against the principalities, powers and rulers of darkness in this world.

First, we are compelled to be a community of hospitality. Over a year ago, the Methodist Church entrusted a large, historic building to our care. The church that once inhabited the building closed down years ago. Through an intense discernment process, Mercy Junction Justice and Peace Center decided that keeping an empty building would be sinful. We open our sanctuary and chapel seven days a week for anyone to find shelter, soup, drink and conversation. By anyone, we mean old, young, homeless, lonely, poor, neighbor, friend, family, refugee, and stranger. We serve food, show silent films, offer a spirituality library, participate in conversation, and deepen our community. Every day, our staff stops to sit and eat together at tables in the middle of the sanctuary. On Wednesday, we gather in a peacemakers circle to debrief and reflect on the meaning of radical hospitality and community. Often, we remind each other that our horizontal relationships with the "least of these" will yield more access to the divine than any of our vertical yearning.

Second, we have small gatherings that attempt to spend some time each day in reflection and meditation. Different groups and people lead us every day at 5:00 pm in a variety of reflections. Since we have a diversity of participants, this service is open to all during the weekdays. On Saturday we participate in our interfaith circle called "The People's Sermon" and on Sunday we have a Christian service called "The Blessing." It is important that we root every aspect of our radical actions in the spirituality connecting us to the divine. It is essential for our community to see each action as an outgrowth of faith and discipleship. Our Protest, as Protestants against all forms of oppression to living creatures, is deeply rooted in a 2000-year-old heritage of resistance that is too often denuded by those who want Christian worship to be safe, inspiring and shallow.

Third, we believe that worship includes radical acts of defiance against principalities, powers and rulers of darkness in this world to bring salvation to all people. For us, salvation is not the individualized notion of going to heaven or worldly success promised by the evangelical movement and our Capitalist society. Preachers have packaged salvation as something that is personal. It has become a commodity that one can own, instead of something that saves our church, community and the world.

By contrast, we understand salvation to be resistance that pushes the trajectory of history toward equality and compassion for all living creatures. At Mercy Junction Justice and Peace Center, we proclaim that salvation is in seeing the world as it ought to be, and agitating hell's principalities until they have been shaken from their perches of power. That begins with our own reflection, meditation, prayer, repentance, and transformation.

> **We understand salvation to be resistance that pushes...toward equality and compassion for all living creatures.**

This is why direct action and mutual aid are so central to our own spiritual growth. These actions put us at risk in ways similar to the constant condition of those who are oppressed. It may be our only opportunity to find Christ in this world. Our responsibility as allies is to use our privilege to fight for justice, peace, equality, mercy and grace in every aspect of our society. This sometimes means fighting the corruption at city hall, a corporate board, or in our denominations. There is a prophetic calling that this age requires for all of creation to survive. We are positioning ourselves to be conduits of that divine grace that burns for a just life in this moment.

What is worship? Worship is meeting to share communion weekly. It is protesting for-profit prisons. It is crying with immigrants suffering abuse. It is physically standing between a transphobic person and a self-identified woman. It is loving politicians who have denied thousands of people healthcare by calling them to account for the harm they have done. It sometimes feels like being betrayed by friends. It is reinterpreting the Bible so that it makes the world into a place for all people. And it is certainly not limited by even our own definitions of worship. Worship is our grateful, angry, comforting, frightened, pleading and joyous response to the divine as a community of faith chosen by God. It is the liturgy of the people. It is always expanding to meet our needs as humans to bring about salvation in the world.

-BM/MC

Be Not Afraid
Rick Ufford-Chase

What does it take to nurture Christian communities whose members collectively embody the daring life of Jesus? This question interests me more than any other I've taken up in this book.

There are plenty of vibrant churches across the United States. However, far too many of those churches have chosen, either consciously or unconsciously, to create a community of faith that reflects dominant culture values. This is, almost always, an attempt to make our churches attractive to greater numbers of adherents.

To my way of thinking, there are two legitimate purposes for the church that professes to follow Jesus. One is to provide a genuine support system for communities of people who have been excluded from the Empire in some way. I think of a little, Pentecostal church called Roca de Salvacion (Rock of Salvation) on the outskirts of Guatemala City that I visited years ago. Most of the members were food insecure, armed gangs ruled their neighborhood, and alcohol and drug addiction were escapist seductions that threatened their families. The small congregation held a prayer meeting, Bible study or worship service every single night of the week to provide support for its members. When I marveled at this demonstration of faithfulness that surpassed anything I had ever seen in my churches in the United States, the pastor assured me that it was quite literally a survival strategy for a people under siege.

I also think of new immigrant worshipping communities I've visited here in the United States, whose members band together in an inhospitable culture both for the sense of safety they feel and because it allows them to rediscover and recover joy through fellowship that is familiar. This is an expression of church as refuge. Similarly, African-American churches have a history of helping their members survive slavery and segregation and intentional marginalization in a culture that has been openly hostile here in the United States. These are legitimate expressions of what it means to be church, though I hasten to add that as such populations gain traction in the dominant culture, their churches run the same risk as any white church does of becoming less and less faithful to the call of the gospel and more and more beholden to the seduction of Empire.

The second purpose for a local congregation is to support its members as they make intentional choices to stand against the dominant culture practices and oppressive political and economic structures which undermine the values they are called to embody. I think here of the Christians in the community of Le Chambon, which defied the Nazis and sheltered Jews in France in the 1930's. Alison's description of Southside Presbyterian Church and its history of providing Sanctuary certainly fits this description as well. These are faith communities that take the call of the gospel seriously, not just for its message of individual liberation or salvation (which the Christian gospel undoubtedly offers), but also for its claim on us to create communities that reflect the "kin-dom" of God.

As I read Brian's story about Mercy Junction, I wonder if it might be a church that actually manages to fulfill both purposes simultaneously. It is a place of refuge for a people at risk in an economic and socio-political structure that is clearly rigged against them, but also a church committed to taking active risks to confront the corrosive societal values that are so antithetical to the teachings of Jesus.

Jesus insisted that it was not just possible but imperative that the people of God form communities that could withstand the pressures of Empire values and offer support for an entirely different way of being. Too many of our communities of faith attempt to reduce the gospel message to pablum, insisting that it is all about "me and my Jesus." The impulse is totally understandable in a culture that attempts to rob us of genuine meaning and purpose, but succumbing to this temptation is an abuse of the Christian gospel.

I understand, and have experienced myself, the power of Jesus to transform my life in very personal ways, to fill me with a sense of meaning and purpose, and to help me avoid or pull back from self-destructive behavior. I am an evangelical. My life has been turned upside down by Jesus, as I have experienced the deep, personal sense that Jesus is calling me to give my life over to God and to the work of God today and every day. Since my junior year in high school, I have made every critical decision in my life by discerning what I believe God is calling me to do. I read scripture with the assumption that it has the power to totally upend my life, and that assumption has been confirmed over and over again.

However, Christians who believe that this is the only or the pinnacle experience of what it means to be a follower of Jesus have missed the most important part of Christian conversion that Jesus has to offer. Churches that intentionally ignore the political implications of the gospel, or refuse to recognize their gospel obligation to challenge injustice, or celebrate the values of the dominant culture as a reward for individual faithfulness: those churches are well shy of hitting the mark set by Jesus. They differ only indistinctly from any other social or cultural club, and they often pose a genuine threat to justice, when they focus their energy on protecting the status quo for those who have attained a measure of power by virtue of their race or class or nationality.

Here too, I have been deeply influenced by Jim Corbett, the philosopher/rancher of the borderlands whose work I cited in Chapter Three. Jim was working on a remarkable manuscript when he died, that was later completed by his close friends Father Ricardo Elford and Daniel Baker, and published under the title,

"Sanctuary for All Life." Here is how Jim reflected in that book on the true meaning of the prophetic faith[1]:

> Most religions provide answers to the plea, 'What can I do to win eternal bliss?' That was The Question in the Hellenistic world in which Christianity first took form, so the gospel was taken as The Answer – the Good News about how to save one's soul and live happily ever after.
>
> This isn't the question that energizes the prophetic faith. For the prophetic faith, revelation unfolds in history, guided by the question, 'How are we to fulfill our covenant, to be a holy people?' And, down through the generations the biblical voice urges, 'In community, seek, do, and study torah.' Where the ethic of individual choices proposes the saint and altruism, the ethic of societal practices proposes the base community and torah. The base community's concern is the walking of the hallowing way (halakah) - to enable its members to serve as co-creators of the Peaceable Kingdom, even if this makes them misfits within the established society of their time and place.

Jim's reflection challenges me to re-imagine the purpose of our faith communities: to stretch toward the vision of "walking the hallowing way." Jim repeatedly insisted that this cannot be done by individuals, but instead must be practiced in community. Moral leadership as a seeking of torah is not something that can be learned and recited. It must be practiced by community as that community seeks to weave a covenant of respect for all life into all that it does.

This is why it is so hard to figure out how to reproduce effective and faithful Christian communities in the heart of the Empire. The churches that seem to reflect Jim's vision are the ones that have chosen, intentionally or unintentionally, to locate themselves where practicing torah – in the way Jim understands it – is non-negotiable.

---

[1] Jim Corbett, *Sanctuary for All Life* (Howler Dog Press, 2005), 168-169.

For instance, the history behind Alison Harrington's story of Southside Presbyterian Church's support for Rosa is rooted in its location on the wrong side of the railroad tracks in a community of people struggling with displacement. It began with Native Americans who came in from the O'odham Nation in the 1920's to look for work. In the 1930's, it was a refuge for Mexican families whose families had been labeled "other" when, at the end of the Mexican American War, the U.S. took nearly half of Mexico's territory. It continued when Central American refugees came north in the 1980's, fleeing the violence of U.S.-funded wars in their countries, and when Mexican economic refugees who were casualties of free trade agreements followed them in the 1990's. Southside didn't have to go looking for a cause, they simply had to be faithful and willing to stick their necks out for the people who knocked on their door. "Doing torah" and "walking of the hallowing way" - as Jim would say - was a practice deeply ingrained in the soul of this community of faith long before the opportunity arose to support Rosa.

And though Mercy Junction's context is different, Brian's description of that congregation makes it clear that the fundamental decision to root itself among people at risk and to wrestle honestly and courageously with the implications of the gospel are the heart of what it truly means to be the church in Chattanooga, Tennessee. The first act was throwing open their doors to the community. Everything else flows from that decision.

Every church's location is unique, but there isn't a church in the United States today that will have to go more than a few miles to discover the communities that exist on the margins of the Empire and the colonized peoples of the underside of the global economy. The problem is not that the needs of those on the margins of the Empire are not identifiable, it is that most of our churches have fully isolated themselves from these communities at risk, and are no longer able to recognize any reality outside of their own. However, the capacity of a congregation to expand its engagement with those on the margins can be recaptured, cultivated, and actively practiced. In almost every community across the country it is possible to identify the line beyond which people of privilege have determined it is not safe to go. Crossing that line is what creating prophetic communities of faith are all about.

Speaking from my own location in the Presbyterian Church, we have often been so ensconced in cocoons of comfort and safety that true faithfulness takes a huge act of daring. Getting out of those cocoons can be harder than getting a camel through the eye of a needle. Resistance to Empire requires moving to the edge of the power structures we live within not just metaphorically, but literally. In this regard, our present moment of transition in the church actually offers a significant opportunity.

Margaret Aymer, Associate Professor of New Testament at Austin Seminary, has turned my reading of the Beatitudes in the book of Matthew on its head. In a Bible study she authored for Horizon's Magazine called "Confessing the Beatitudes," Margaret suggested that the traditional interpretation "Blessed are you" that begins each verse in Matthew should more rightly be translated "Greatly Honored are you." Her translation gets to the heart of the social location Jesus had in mind for his own community[2]:

> *Greatly honored are the destitute in spirit, for of them is the empire of heaven.*
> *Greatly honored are those who are in mourning, for they will be comforted.*
> *Greatly honored are those who are humbled, for they will inherit the earth.*
> *Greatly honored are those who are famished and parched for justice, for they will be satisfied.*
> *Greatly honored are those who are full of 'chesed' (Hebrew: loving-kindness), for they will receive 'chesed'.*

---

[2] Margaret Aymer, "Confessing the Beatitudes," *Horizons* (Louisville: Presbyterian Women, Inc., 2011)

Greatly honored are the pure of heart, for they will see God.
Greatly honored are those who make 'shalom', for they will be
called sons of God.
Greatly honored are those who are persecuted for the sake of
justice, for of them is the empire of God.
Greatly honored are y'all when people revile y'all and persecute
y'all and say all kinds of evil against y'all falsely on my account.
Rejoice and be glad for your reward is great in heaven for in the
same way they persecuted the prophets who were before y'all.

There's plenty to unpack here, and Margaret's Bible study is well worth the time, but the bottom line is that this vision of community is, at its heart, what Jim was talking about when he described "base communities" that are willing to commit to the practice of the torah. These are the values of the new community, the community that offers shalom in place of the military-imposed pax Romana, and the community that invests in the Empire of heaven as a clear alternative to the destructive values of the Empire on earth.

Our greatest gift as we attempt to give up the privileges of the church of Empire to become communities of resistance is also the threat with which most of our churches have become obsessed: the fear of dying. Fifty years ago it would have been impossible to imagine more than a handful of churches taking this challenge seriously, precisely because we were so firmly ensconced in the matrix of power. Our churches were planted on the corners of most town squares and our tall-steeple churches were filled with the captains of industry. We were the decision makers. At our best, we were the moral conscience of the nation lifting up a social gospel to stem the excesses of capitalism. At our worst, we accommodated ourselves to the glitter and false promise of Empire, and molded our interpretation of the Bible to suit our accommodation.

In 2016, that luxury is gone for all but a few of our churches. Most of our children (and many of our colleagues and friends as well) see no need for church, which was only filled with pious people and a message about being "good" that could be filled with individual expressions of spirituality anyway. Our numbers are dwindling fast, and those of us who remain have, by necessity, become obsessed with meeting budgets that will maintain buildings built for a different era. Here's the honest and uncomfortable truth. By any reasonable measure, there are far more "at-risk" congregations than there are "healthy" congregations. I put these words in quotations because in my experience our estimation of what constitutes "at-risk" and "healthy" are diametrically opposed to gospel values.

Even the churches that think they are still healthy and vibrant today are, in my experience, only a few years away from teetering on the brink of disaster as well. It is such an irony that we are churches filled with many wealthy people (a few years ago, we Presbyterians surpassed the Episcopalians as the wealthiest denomination per capita), yet we act as if we can't afford to be church. The problem is not that people are not giving, it is that we are maintaining the mechanics of an institution built for a bygone era.

Our instinct in such a moment is understandable, but dead wrong. Most of us are fearful, and the most fundamental value we have internalized is not to do anything that will make anyone else uncomfortable enough to leave. We tell ourselves that something is too "political" to be discussed, when what we really mean is that we are afraid to challenge the status quo. We are not interested in inhabiting the dangerous space on the margins of the Empire. This impulse may be understandable, but it is better suited to running a country club than it is to sustaining a church.

So how do we start again? How do we support the congregations that are genuinely interested in being the body of Christ? Is it possible to continue to provide care for those who are not ready to abandon the church of Empire, without getting sucked into the trap of catering to a perversion of the gospel that is patently contrary to the teachings and the life of Jesus? What would it look like to nurture a renewed movement of communities that commit, as Jim says, "to seek, do and study torah."

During the years of the Sanctuary movement in which he was such a pivotal figure, Jim constructed a set of principles to guide local communities as they took up the dangerous work of defying the U.S. Government and responding directly to the needs of Central American refugees. He called the principles "Civil Initiative," and specifically envisioned them as a way for civilian populations to responsibly protect basic human rights when those rights are being abused by the government. I have discovered them to be remarkably useful in forming Christian communities that are committed to active resistance to the ways of Empire[3].

- The church in resistance must commit to nonviolence. Jim often said that the nonviolent protection of human rights is never illegal, regardless of what the power brokers and governments of the Empire may insist. This happens to be in line with Jesus' own teachings, and it is particularly useful when the church is concerned with taking on the abuses of Empire that are backed with overwhelming military might. Ironically, as Jesus appeared to know so well, there is no way to beat such power brokers at their own game, but the power of small communities committed to nonviolence often flummoxes the powers that be.

- We must commit to be truthful. There can be nothing hidden or discreet about our efforts. Transparency keeps us honest, and assures that we are willing to pay the cost for our resistance. This is especially true in situations like the United States where there is – at least in theory – a democratic system of governance and intact rule of law.

---

[3] Adapted from: Jim Corbett, "Principles of Civil Initiative," *The Sanctuary Church* (Wallingford, PA: Pendle Hill), 23-24.

- Jim said that our efforts must be catholic, by which he meant that we cannot distinguish between those we will aid based on their origin or religious belief. This, at the end of the day, is the best response to those who would use Christian identity as a bludgeon to determine who is "in" and who is "out" in our communities and nation.

- Our efforts must be germane to the actual needs of those who are without power in the Empire project – the colonized, the global factory worker, the migrant or refugee, those who do not carry privilege in a system of white supremacy. Our goal is, wherever possible, to respond to the actual needs of all God's people (by which I mean – all people). When we find ourselves advocating through choreographed acts of civil disobedience or through political advocacy that is disembodied and disconnected from the needs of those most affected, we should check our assumptions and proceed only with great caution. It seems to me that this is what Ched Myers has in mind when he insists that our first act must be to locate ourselves in a specific watershed and begin to restore that place. It is certainly what Southside had in mind when they offered sanctuary to Rosa for more than a year. This is not a show for public attention. Any attention our act of "being church" brings to the creation or practice of public policy should be intended, but ancillary.

- We must maintain relationships with those with whom we disagree. In Jim's words, Civil Initiative is dialogical. We must always assume that our ideas can be tested by those with whom we disagree, which offers the possibility for seeking common ground.

- Jim insisted that the basic protection of human rights, which I have extended to the practice of being church, must be "volunteer-based." What he meant, at least in part, was that the professionalization of our work eventually necessitates the creation of institutions that must maintain themselves for their own sake – eventually becoming the point of the entire exercise. Though it is personally painful for me to say, I believe that this is one of the fundamental challenges to our understanding of what it means to be the church in the United States today, and I will have much more to say about it in each of the chapters to come.

- Finally, the principles of Civil Initiative must be practiced in community. This cannot be about one person choosing to act as a lone ranger, however significant that person's response or ministry may be. The ideas and practice of our work are tested in the crucible of our local, faith community. This keeps us accountable and it sustains us for the long haul. Remember Alison's story of what was demanded of the members of the church in their practice of Sanctuary: the "solidarity suite" that housed dozens of volunteers who stayed with Rosa in the church, and the practice that the congregation instituted of nightly prayer vigils to sustain the work over time were critically important to the effort.

So, what does it take to nurture Christian communities that are capable of actually embodying the life of Jesus? Here's the good news. It doesn't cost a lot of money. In fact, money appears to make it harder, not easier, to follow the way of Jesus. And it doesn't demand a lot of people. On the contrary, small communities are the ones that seem to have the greatest ability to summon the collective courage to resist. Resistance to the powers and the principalities has always been nurtured in the communities where the people of God appear to have nothing left to lose.

Hmmm. Sounds like a lot of the churches I see today

-RUC

Discussion Questions:

1. What is your response to Margaret Aymer's translation of the Beatitudes? How does it change your understanding of what Jesus was trying to help his followers understand?

2. Rick and Brian are insisting that locating ourselves with the people who are most beaten down in our society is the first act of any faithful church. Have you experienced the kind of faith community they are describing? What was it like?

3. What do you think of Brian's answer to his own question - "What is worship?" How would you answer the question?

4. Reread Rick's description of the principles of Civil Initiative and discuss the implications of each.

Chapter 7
Theological Education As An Act Of Subversion

Taking back the Church
Laura Newby, Jin S. Kim, and John Nelson

In 2014, Church of All Nations launched Underground Seminary, a two-year, immersive, alternative seminary experience focused on character formation, a comprehensive understanding of how power works in the world, and a decolonized reading of the Bible. Our curriculum is informed by the needs and experiences of our people at Church of All Nations, a multicultural, multiethnic, and multigenerational PC(USA) congregation in Minneapolis, Minnesota.

Since our congregation's founding, we have coalesced as family by telling our diverse stories and exploring our particular histories together. Through vulnerable testimony, we partake in each other's pain and struggles, and after years of this deep sharing we have discovered a common root to many of our traumas.

Whether black or white, female or male, Native American, recent immigrant or colonial settler, the root of oppression for so many in this country seems to be Western imperialism. Our members include refugees from war, descendants of slaves, indigenous survivors of genocide, and immigrants whose communal ways of life are disintegrating in the face of Western individualism. We are seeing how our many problems, both structural and personal, have their roots in American Empire.

Our people hunger to make sense of the world. They yearn for faith leaders to understand and articulate what they experience. They want their struggles validated, and they seek a place to grieve their pain without judgment. They long for a community that challenges the status quo and works for systemic change, and hope that another way of life is possible. Our people yearn for a church that is more than formal religiosity, empty piety, institutional self-preservation, and transactional in its ways of relating. They want a healthy church that is also intimate family. In short, our people want a community that embodies good news.

At Church of All Nations we are united as a Christian community in our resistance to the logic of Empire and by our faith in Jesus Christ to overcome it. We seek to decolonize ourselves from the imperial impulse to control and dominate, so that the Holy Spirit can lead us to true salvation.

As our community evolved over the years, we began to ask who is equipping Christian leaders for this kind of ministry. Who is helping them to clearly see the imperial context that corrupts us all and to root out the neuroses of Empire from within themselves? Who is making sure our theology students recognize the socio-political teaching at the heart of Jesus' ministry? Who is teaching them to see the glaringly obvious parallels between Palestine in New Testament times and the world of American Empire in our time? Who is teaching them to lead creatively and courageously, to understand, imagine and construct the peaceable kingdom here on earth? Who is teaching our people to expose imperial propaganda, to subvert Empire rather than go along with it? Where do they learn to be as shrewd as a serpent with

Who is teaching our people to...subvert Empire rather than go along with it?

the powers that be while being as innocent as a dove before God?

When Pastor Jin was in seminary in the early 1990s, it took him a long time to make sense of what he saw among his classmates. The African-American students seemed to know that the theological education they were getting was largely irrelevant – whitewashed and steeped in Platonism. They had to jump through white institutional and theological hoops to get the credentialing necessary to advance in ministry or the academy. They did what they had to do, but returned to their communities where their real education resumed. The Asian-American students studied this white systematic theology a bit more naively, but most didn't internalize it the way the white students did. Both the African-American and Asian-American students retained a non-western sensibility that kept them from fully buying into theological abstraction.

As a response to this professionalized approach to ministry, Church of All Nations began an internship program in 2005. On one hand, these pastoral interns, in the middle of the typical seminary-to-ministry pipeline, wanted Church of All Nations to give them a unique internship experience that would put them ahead of the competition. On the other, they were open to profound disruption in their path to professionalized ministry. What we discovered was that it often took a full year just to deprogram them from the expectations of a middle class lifestyle and a lifelong career protected and nurtured by the clerical guild we call our governing bodies.

Much of the two to three years of this internship was spent on discipleship and character formation. As these interns began to experience life together in an intimate community, to deal honestly with themselves and their past, and to connect with people on a level that was deep and sometimes scary, ministry became real. It was not a thing to do or make a living off of, but a way of life into which we invite others. They learned that authentic ministry was pastoral, prophetic and evangelical.

The many interns who have been trained here have without exception recognized both the woeful inadequacy of the standard theological education they received and their own lack of seriousness in the study required to be an effective pastor in this complex age. They were hungry to learn the Bible from a counter-imperial perspective, to understand history, and to grasp how political, social and economic systems actually work in the world. They wanted to comprehend the invisible structures that endlessly oppress people, and why the church seemed powerless in the face of such powers and principalities.

Our seminary graduates, just like our people, were crying out for more understanding and transformation. Where could people go who wanted to be deprogrammed from the dominant culture? Or for those whose calling did not necessitate accreditation by a denominational body? What about those who would like to be ordained in the PC(USA) but no longer feel the time, money and conventional education are worth it? And what do we do with those who cannot afford to pile on massive amounts of seminary debt on top of college debt?

Not satisfied with the existing options for theological education, we thought a more effective way to equip Christian leaders than through our post-MDiv internship was to start a seminary ourselves. This experiment we call Underground Seminary.

We have a one-cohort-at-a-time model, an intensive immersion experience in which students earn their MDiv in two years. Our curriculum consists of three tracks: Unveiling, Reimagining, and Birthing. During our first eight-month trimester, Unveiling, we study anthropology, world history, global economics, and politics. This helps us to see the big picture, through which we attempt to locate ourselves in history. An overarching juxtaposition that frames much of our learning is the spectrum between indigeneity and imperialism. Is the recovery of ancient indigenous values key to the recovery of our own humanity? What can we learn from the struggle between indigenous and imperial values evident in the Scriptures? How can the church be a locus to practice humanity?

Our second trimester reimagines the world as God intended it to be by reading the Bible from a post-imperial lens. The third trimester involves internalizing all that we've learned, integrating it holistically, and taking concrete steps toward constructive ministry.

All of this is done while embedded in our very active congregational life. We constantly reflect on our life together, from happenings in the church to the intersection of national and global events. Our students live together in an intentional community home led by one of the instructors. We meet in the mornings for class, cook lunch together, read the following day's material, and then work together on a project. We regularly practice hospitality. All of our students are involved in at least one church ministry. Though every class discussion includes personal engagement with the material, once a week we set aside time to process how we're relating with each other, the church community, and our families of origin. Our students are expected to grow in self-differentiation and to understand the family systems dynamic that shaped their identity. This is for the purpose of genuine discipleship that can actually change the world.

-LN/JSK/JN

A Pedagogy of Resistance
Rick Ufford-Chase

If you've made it this far into the book, I'm going to assume that you are on board with my general thesis: the church of tomorrow will have to look remarkably different than the church of today, and getting there is likely to be an enterprise that involves a great deal of daring behavior. So, what kind of theological education is going to get us there?

Put another way, what would theological formation look like if it was seen as a lifelong habit and preparation for living in resistance to the Empire? How would that look different from theological education designed primarily as a vocational preparation for the professional ministerial class?

Before attempting an answer to this question, I want to offer a disclaimer.

I have good friends who have given their lives to the task of building strong seminaries to educate our

> What would theological formation look like if it was seen as a lifelong habit and preparation for living in resistance to the Empire?

ministers. Many of them are innovators who experiment with all kinds of creative initiatives to create educational opportunities that are finely attuned to the church of tomorrow. Further, I have been shaped and formed in significant ways by the thinking that has been done in those institutions.

I am not trying to make the case that we should disband all of our theological institutions. I am being intentionally provocative. I am not a part of the academy, and have no responsibility for maintaining the theological institutions that have been the backbone of the church for more than a century. On the other hand, I have a lot of love for the institutions of our church and I have invested significant energy in supporting some of them to retool so that they might thrive in the future. I offer these judgments as a colleague interested in engendering thoughtful debate, and with the hope of inspiring us to rethink the fundamental assumptions we have made about ministry and about what it means to be the church.

Taking on the question of what theological formation would look like if it was seen as a lifelong habit and preparation for living in resistance to Empire requires some key judgments about what the shape of Christian community is likely to be a few years into the future. Here are my assumptions:

In the future, few congregations will be able to afford full-time, professional pastors. Leadership will be largely in the hands of the laity, and ministers will spend most of their time on the formation and nurture of lay people who will lead the church. I expect that the commitment to theological study will be carried as a *charism* by certain members of our congregations who commit to that education as a way to fulfill a special role in their community. This is likely to be no different than many other spiritual gifts that might be offered by members of the faith community. For example, some are skilled at providing pastoral care for the community. Others might dedicate time for direct service with folks who are homeless. Still others might be tapped to teach or to develop resources to enrich the worship life of the community. It is ironic that, as we diminish our reliance on ministers for our theological study and guidance, people with a particular interest in and aptitude for theological study are likely to become more important to the entire community.

As the entire community takes on the vocation of "being church" together, there will be fewer and fewer opportunities for full-time, dedicated ministers to find employment. This is already happening, of course, so it's not as if one needs a crystal ball to see the future. There will be space for people who dedicate themselves primarily to the work of the church or the faith community, but our notions of how those dedicated persons will sustain themselves and their families will be dramatically different.

Many of the rules we have put in place regarding minimum salaries, paid vacation and retirement benefits have been designed by the corporate church to mirror the corporate economy in the United States. The problem is that those values, though they harmonize well with the high value our culture places on self-reliance, do not reflect any biblical mandate that I can think of. Nowhere in the gospel does it say "pay your religious leaders well so that they will not be a burden on the community," but our scripture repeatedly references the value of communities whose members care for one another and provide for one another's needs.

This is at the heart of Jim Corbett's principle that our practice of "being church" (my term, not Jim's) must be a volunteer effort. When I arrived on the border in 1987 as a young adult volunteer, I was invited to live in a group house with four other young adults. The bills were paid by the fundraising efforts of the Tucson refugee support group, allowing our young adult crew to serve as full-time volunteers and to take on a great deal of the responsibility for interviewing and accompanying Central American Refugees as they came north, getting them across the border, and coordinating their travel to safe churches around the country. The fundraising we took on as a community to help us cover our expenses actually took very little time or energy because we lived together and because we were so intentional about keeping our expenses low.

When we were starting BorderLinks a few years later, we created an intentional community in which a few of our members handled the bulk of our housing expense, allowing others to work full time in border advocacy and education efforts. All of us understood that we were supporting important work together, and I don't remember there being dissension or resentment. In my more recent experience, the Community of Living Traditions at Stony Point Center is made up of volunteers whose basic needs are taken care of by the Conference Center. It's a win-win situation, where the support of the conference center allows our multifaith residential volunteers to focus significant amounts of time on the intentional effort that goes into creating a healthy, multifaith community and shaping our shared commitment to justice and peace work in the world around us. Simultaneously, the conference center receives remarkable "value added" from a group of passionate volunteers who support the operation of the business and create a community culture that enriches the experience of our guests.

The point is that we are going to have to extract ourselves from decades of effort we have put into the professionalization of the church. It's not affordable. It's not sustainable. It's not biblical. In the end, it's not even desirable. It's hard to give witness to a counter-culture message when we have been entirely co-opted by an ethic better designed for corporate enterprise. There is much I appreciate about the experience of the Church of All Nations, but one of the things I most appreciate is their lived understanding of this reality, wherein the students live together with several members of the church who carry most of the responsibility for the household economy.

An important side effect to this shift away from a professional class of ministers is that astronomical debt accumulated in process of acquiring a degree will be unacceptable. It's not that we will not want or need some members of our community to have developed the discipline of rigorous theological study and reflection. Rather, seminaries will have to find new ways to adopt counter-cultural practices of supporting their students - spiritually, emotionally, and economically. The seminary experience will need to offer students the opportunity to learn the skills of less-expensive, communal living: skills that are not easy to hone in our cultural and economic context. Those skills will likely be transferrable to the specific ministries in which most of our theologically trained leaders with find themselves: rural communities, cities, even suburban contexts increasingly lend themselves to this kind of counter-cultural living.

Further, local faith communities will be much more connected to seminary students, since theological education will be geared largely toward committed lay people who are firmly rooted in their own faith communities. This offers the opportunity for the sending community to share the responsibility for the cost of their own candidates for theological education. I expect that discerning whether someone is called to this level of theological preparation will become a far more profound community experience rather than an individual exploration, with the goal of discerning who in the community has a special gift for study that can be developed into a teaching skill to benefit the whole community. If, as Ched Myers suggests, we couple these ideas with a new commitment to inhabit a specific watershed over many years, then it will make much more sense for seminary education to be a shared commitment of the entire community.

Another assumption that shapes my thinking about theological education in the future is that our practice of worship will change dramatically. Though I believe the fundamental theology behind our carefully constructed worship will stay the same (calling us to worship, confessing our sins before God and one another, engaging the Word, sharing the grounding ritual of communion, and supporting and lifting one another up in prayer), how we worship will look very different than it has traditionally. I've visited the Church of All Nations and experienced the personal testimonies that the pastoral staff reference in their essay as they reflect on what led them to start the Underground Seminary. This worshipful practice, often experienced in evangelical churches but largely lost in many of the more traditional protestant churches, should be the foundational experience of our communities because it will deepen our understanding and appreciation for one another far more than our current worship practices do. What really makes this practice meaningful at the Church of All Nations is that the staff is trained and skilled at drawing out the political implications of personal stories, transforming this from an exercise in self-centeredness into a deeply meaningful community critique of the dominant culture values that are beating down their members and challenging them in their practice of Christian community.

However, the transformation of our understanding of worship isn't likely to stop there. The art of communicating a theologically grounded message will move away from one-way, didactic preaching styles and toward far more interactive and tactile engagement of the text that can only be done effectively in small groups. As we all become more adept at interacting with scripture, I expect that social media will play a much greater role in theological literacy, making ideas that were once accessible only with years of theological study much more available to the members of our religious communities. Instead of spending hours each week crafting a sermon (an educational pedagogy that has fewer and fewer proponents as our members vote with their feet and spend their Sunday mornings elsewhere), we will move toward new ways of engaging the text similar to the "Circle of Praxis" developed by Latin American communities who were called to resist the brutal military juntas and powerful economic oligarchies during the 1970's and 1980's.

The circle of praxis, modified from the educational theories of Paulo Freire, is quite simple in its construction, yet radical in its impact. Most church-goers in Latin America were Catholic at that time, and most Catholic Masses were still in Latin. Far from being encouraged to engage the text, most parishioners were actively discouraged from doing so. Following the Second Vatican Council in 1964 and the Catholic Council at Medellin of 1968 that denounced wide-scale poverty across Latin America as sin, some priests and nuns began to create small circles of study called "Christian Base Communities." (This is the foundation for Jim Corbett's use of the term "base communities" in Sanctuary for All Life.) The idea was simple and powerful. Anyone who is capable of reading the text, or hearing the text read, and reflecting on their lived experience, is "doing theology." The circle of praxis laid out the basic cycle: to observe one's situation, to read the text and reflect on its meaning in light of one's lived reality, and to take action together to address the implications of the text.

It is not hard to understand why the campesinos saw such a concept as liberating. They could immediately intuit the connections between the message of Jesus in the Bible and the oppressive conditions in which they were living. Likewise, it is easy to understand how such an activity could have been seen as radical and subversive by those who sought to protect the status quo. The similarities between the temple priest's relationship to the officials of the Roman Empire in first century Palestine and the Catholic hierarchy's allegiance to the military regimes of Nicaragua, Guatemala, Colombia and El Salvador in the 1980's were not lost on the radical priests and nuns (and a few courageous Bishops) who promoted this empowering theology.

I believe that this understanding of theology is likely to experience a resurgence over the next generation, largely due to the convergence of three factors. First, our churches will continue to become much smaller, either intentionally or unintentionally. In my own small church of 30 members in Stony Point, NY, we have been without an installed pastor for nearly two years, but I would argue that the theological engagement of our members has actually deepened substantially as we have been forced to take responsibility for our own worship life. Nothing has the potential to shake us from complacency quite like the need to survive, though I'm amazed at the number of congregations who hold tightly to their complacency to the bitter end.

Second, access to the Internet places good theological scholarship at our fingertips as we wrestle with the text. For several years, the Christian cohort of the Community of Living Traditions at Stony Point Center has been meeting each Sunday morning at 8 a.m. for "Bible and Bagels." Though no one prepares ahead of time, each week our conversation is rich as we explore the implications of the lectionary text. Several among us hold seminary degrees (and lately we've even been blessed by the presence of Norman Gottwald, the Christian Scholar renowned for his study of the Hebrew Scriptures), but an easy give and take occurs as we all explore ideas together.

We often stumble into new thinking that captures our imaginations as some of us follow the thread of an idea on the Internet in the midst of the conversation. The depth of the conversation rivals the kind of engagement I felt with my classmates during my brief stint at Princeton Theological Seminary thirty years ago.

Third, we are blessed – and challenged – by a younger generation of skeptics who are in no way interested in the pronouncements of "experts." This generation of doubters, raised on the internet, are savvy and adept at spotting charlatans, fakes, and hypocrites. Listening to a pastor preach week after week without allowing for significant pushback is not a pedagogy in which they have any interest. Further, listening to a radical gospel read from the pulpit while seeing little evidence that the members of our congregations are addressing the fundamental challenges of the text gives lie to our claim to be church. While this skepticism prevails among young adults, it certainly is not limited to them. Plenty of my friends, who were raised in the church as I was, have long since given up on participating in traditional worship in any real way. Many of them simply cannot see significant value in the exercise. We have a habit of placing the blame on such naysayers themselves, claiming that "church isn't what we do for us, it is what we do for God." Such accusations ring hollow when our discipline of being church so often appears to be more about institutional preservation than a genuine desire to witness to the challenging demands of Jesus to "feed my sheep."

Yet another assumption about the future of church is that many (and maybe even most) of our congregations will choose to get out of the property management business that they increasingly find themselves in as they rent space to other churches or community organizations in an effort to pay the bills. Instead, they will choose to focus their limited energy in far more important and personally engaging ways as they commit to what it will take to build far more meaningful expressions of community. Put another way, communities that dedicate themselves to the kinds of challenges laid out in this book are likely to find themselves consumed with the vocation of being church, whatever their day jobs may be. Unless we can see the usefulness of our buildings as an integral part of what it means to take on the significant challenges of our time, many of us will eventually come to the inevitable conclusion that the bricks and mortar are weighing us down, however obligated we may feel to our forebears who entrusted those buildings to us.

Ironically, I personally find this extremely challenging. I have spent a lifetime trying to protect the resources of the institution, and have always believed that once we let go of these remarkable properties, we are never likely to get them back. Further, many of our congregations feel a legitimate sense of responsibility for what may take place in their neighborhoods if they abandon their building, which seems like a fair concern so long as the congregants themselves haven't long since abandoned those same neighborhoods. However, if maintaining the buildings for their own sake has become the primary focal point of our ministry, then those buildings have become idols that actually impede our ability to do the work we are called to do. The biblical judgment on idols is pretty clear. If it were easy to do away with the idols, which is clearly what God demands of us, they wouldn't be idols in the first place.

So if these are some of the primary marks of what it will mean to be church over the next fifty years, what are the skills that we will need to develop in our leaders? I think the pastoral staff of the Church of All Nations and the students of the Underground Seminary get it right. In spite of all of our best efforts to the contrary, we still prepare our theological students primarily for the task of institutional protection and assimilation in the Empire. Contrary to all visible evidence that such an exercise is unsustainable, we still appear to begin with the expectation that somehow the local congregation will have both the sense of obligation and the financial means to offer a professional salary to provide for our pastors' families in a way that offers all the privileges of dominant culture lifestyle.

Instead, we should be developing theological education that focuses on the skills our leaders will need to nurture Christian communities of resistance.

- The next generation of leaders will need to know how to manage the significant conflict that is an unavoidable part of every authentic experience of community (a topic for another book).

- They will need to be multilingual and have the ability to navigate cultural difference, which will demand they demonstrate their own cultural humility as an integral part of providing leadership.

- They will need to be far more rigorous in their reading of the gospel from the perspective of the church in opposition to Empire as opposed to the church that operates as apologist for the Empire.

- They will need to be organizers and activists, and be skilled at reading the political signs of the times. They will need to know how to lift up others and how to let go of the power and prestige that has become an expected benefit for pastors.

- They will need to be skilled communicators, with a clear knowledge of how to find other, like-minded communities with whom to make common cause.

- They will need to be wise about the major challenges confronting the church today. The work of confronting white supremacy and decolonizing our church, taking on violence and watershed discipleship, and creating a genuinely inclusive church that stands against fear: these are tall orders, and they demand savvy, well-educated leaders who are willing to root themselves in a particular place for the long haul.

And those are just the marks of the skill sets that will be needed for the critical work of congregational formation. Many of our pastors will also need to become multi-vocational as a matter of economic survival for both their own families and for the congregations they serve. Some seminaries have already been breaking new ground in this direction.

So what will it look like to offer theological education that develops this new generation of non-traditional leaders for our faith communities? There is clearly no one, correct answer, but here are a few steps in the right direction, some of which I have touched on above.

1. **We must develop partnerships with seminaries around the world.**

   The world is far smaller than it was a generation ago. The most effective way to help aspiring leaders who have grown up – as I have – to challenge the easy assumptions of the privileges of Empire is to spend significant time studying the bible, thinking theologically, and examining global socio economic realities together with those who have grown up outside the Empire, or on the margins of the Empire here in the United States. Many U.S. seminaries now have relationships with sister institutions in the Global South. Every student should be spending some significant time studying outside the cultural context in which they have been raised. This will have the added benefit of helping students learn second or even third languages and become familiar with the sending cultures of many of the people who make up our communities across the United States today.

2. **We should look to the practice - cultivated in many other countries - wherein we support leaders who feel a sense of calling from within our congregations and then send them for training in the skills they will need to employ back in their home congregation or community.**

There are many models for providing low-cost, highly sophisticated theological education that is oriented toward such pastors, who typically do not have the luxury of leaving their job, their family, or their congregation for a three year course of study. My favorites - only because I have had direct experience of them - are The Evangelical Center for Pastoral Studies in Central America (CEDEPCA - based in Guatemala), New York Theological Seminary (based in Manhattan), and the Newark School of Theology. (I encourage you to check out these three, but there are dozens of examples of alternative models.)

3. **We're going to need to let go of some of our most beloved buildings.**

The cost of maintaining our buildings is bankrupting our seminaries and putting the cost of theological education way out of reach for far too many people who want access to it. Even the seminaries that have significant endowments should, at the very least, be asking themselves the question whether maintaining these properties is an expression of faithfulness in a world where vast income disparity places all of our communities at significant risk. Perhaps our theological institutions should be actively moving to the margins as well, inhabiting warehouses or farms or rural or urban churches that can no longer keep their doors open.

4. **Our curriculum will need to be far more holistic in its attempt to create leadership for communities of resistance to the Empire.**

   The Underground Seminary is as good an example as I can think of, but we should also be looking toward Catholic Worker or other intentional communities as partners for teaching what it means to live in faithful defiance of the dominant culture. Our pastoral leadership must be able to model such strategies and support others in their communities as they attempt to form communities that more closely conform to those described in the book of Acts and in Paul's letters to the early church. Such things can't be fully explored in an academic classroom. The art form is to create space to try things out and an academic context that invites honest theological reflection on our attempts as we go along.

5. **There will be as much emphasis on personal integrity and character formation as there is on academic preparation.**

   Why does this matter? Because living with integrity in the context of the American ethos of Empire is actually more important than any other aspect of ministry today. We are surrounded by a people who are deeply cynical about the exercise of power, and they have every right to their cynicism. Christian communities must offer a meaningful alternative to the empty promises that bombard our people every day, and that starts with developing leaders who are prepared to take a stand unequivocally on the side of the gospel. In my estimation, this is a primary driver for the loss of the next generation. Let's offer something real and see what happens.

I find the prospect of helping to re-imagine theological education as thrilling as anything I can imagine. It must be faithful to the values of the gospel. It will feel organic because it will be far more closely connected to committed communities of resistance. It will be academically rigorous and playful and honest and imaginative and bold. This is our time, and this is too important a conversation for us be anything less than fully engaged!

-RUC

Discussion Questions:

1. Reread the essay by Jin Kim, Laura Newby and John Nelson that opened this chapter. How does it change your understanding of what theological education should be?

2. Rick's assumptions about how churches will change are necessarily incomplete. What would you add to his list as you imagine what faithful communities will look like over the next twenty years.

3. Are there things in this chapter that make you uncomfortable or anxious? Rick's opening statement was that he is being intentionally provocative, which begs an honest and passionate discussion.

4. The Document Rick references that was created nearly fifty years ago at the Catholic Bishops Council at Medellin, Colombia is relatively short. http://www.shc.edu/theolibrary/resources/medpov.htm. How do you think this document would have been received at the time it was written? What might it have to say to us today?

Chapter 8
Mission as a Move to the Margins

Standing With El Tamarindo
By Linda Eastwood with Germán Zárate

As the sun rose over the scattering of simple homes and farm-plots on this supposedly protected "humanitarian zone," the riot police lined up to ensure that there would be no resistance to the bulldozers and the hired hands entering to start the day's demolition and clearance. The bulldozers and armed support (legal or otherwise) had come again and again, over the years, to violently destroy the homes and crops of the farming community of El Tamarindo near the north-coast city of Barranquilla, Colombia. Every member of this group had already faced violent displacement from other parts of Colombia, but their legal claim to stay on this land they had cultivated over many years was being ignored. At each threat to the community, allies were there alongside and behind the scenes, supporting, documenting, and advocating. The community of El Tamarindo, like the persistent widow of Luke 18:1-8 wearing down the unjust judge, knew how to struggle for their rights; they had formed ASOTRACAMPO as a grassroots association of people who work the land to do just that. But how much better if Luke's widow had benefited from allies in the struggle? ASOTRACAMPO had sought out allies in groups such as Fellowship of Reconcilation's Peace Presence and Colombia's Comisión Intereclesial de Justicia y Paz, and in the Presbyterian Church of Colombia (IPC – Iglesia Presbiteriana de Colombia). And through the IPC, Presbyterians from the USA, too, had come to see members of this community not as victims, but as protagonists in their own struggle, and as friends.

Presbyterian links between the U.S. and Colombia date back to the first U.S. missionary in 1856. There have been many deeply-loved U.S. mission co-workers over the years, while more recent Presbytery-to-Presbytery links have deepened the relationships. But the greatest growth in person-to-person relationships dates from 2004, when the Presbyterian Church of Colombia sent a simple request to the Presbyterian Church (USA): Our lives are being threatened because of our work with victims of violence by both state and non-state actors, and your presence alongside us would keep us safer. Please come. Just be with us.

An apparently simple request, but how could we carry it out? It fit neither the paradigms, nor the budget, nor the security concerns of "normal" PC(USA) mission work. Enter the Presbyterian Peace Fellowship (PPF), an independent network of peacemakers whose work started with World War II and conscientious objection, and had grown to include the relevant experience of human-rights accompaniment in 1980's Central America. The Colombia Accompaniment Program began as a three-way partnership between the Presbyterian Peace Fellowship, the Presbyterian Church (USA) and the Presbyterian Church of Colombia. Anne Barstow, a volunteer with the Presbyterian Peace Fellowship, called in help from friends in Witness for Peace and in Peace Brigades International (two human rights organizations working in Colombia) to develop training to prepare pairs of volunteers to "be alongside" in Colombia for a month at a time. The first accompaniers traveled to Colombia within months. They assembled a vanguard for a "ministry of presence" which has continued now for over a decade, and has involved well over a hundred accompaniers.

What do accompaniers do? Our most important role is simply to be there – to see and be seen as a protective presence for entire communities. We are also listeners. We listen to the stories of people who have been violently forced off their land, and declared worthless, by a system that values the megaprojects of agribusiness and extractive industries

> ❝ **We listen to the stories of people who have been ...declared worthless.**

(often foreign companies extracting petroleum or minerals from the land) over the livelihoods of small farmers. The drug trade has complicated the picture, but it is still fundamentally about land. "Just listening" is a strong statement of solidarity, of valuing individuals and their stories. We soon realized that our Colombian partners were intentionally turning our accompaniers into "tellers of stories;" into people who could not only recount the difficult and untold stories of how U.S. foreign policy has supported militarization and violence in Colombia, but could also make those stories personal – stories of their new-found friends. Understanding those stories led us, at the urging of the IPC, to advocate for change with both the U.S. and Colombian governments.

Even before the request for accompaniment in 2004, the IPC in 2000 appealed for the PC(USA) to raise their voices against U.S. military aid to Colombia. They used the Biblical model of Esther. "When Mordecai was desperate about the danger to the Jewish people, he asked Queen Esther not to keep silent. For the same reason we ask you not to keep silent." That letter pointed out the responsibility of those of us in the U.S. to use our privileged positions as voters, to advocate, and to lobby for our Colombian friends. In the Reformed tradition, we believe that God elects us "for service as well as salvation," and calls us "to work for the transformation of society by seeking justice."

This brings us back to El Tamarindo, where the police stand guard and bulldozers wait to clear homes and farms, and the community members resist their displacement as a result of Colombia's armed conflict. One 78 year-old told us it was his fifth experience of forced displacement. Facing such long odds, our partners in the Presbyterian Church of Colombia have taught us to become advocates on their behalf as they moved to address the underlying causes of the violence. In 2007, as the Colombian Government was laying the groundwork for a U.S.-Colombia Free Trade Agreement that was eventually ratified in 2011, the land inhabited by El Tamarindo was declared a "zona franca," or "free-trade zone." This had a huge impact on the community members as their land shifted from being considered derelict and unwanted to becoming a highly valuable commodity for foreign corporations.

We had advocated with the U.S. government against the terms of the Free Trade Agreement. Now we were also asked to engage in more directly-targeted advocacy with various levels of the Colombian government, and using our well-established relationship with the human-rights section of the U.S. Embassy, to try to ensure that the residents of El Tamarindo were not displaced without receiving compensatory agricultural lands. Our commitment throughout was to follow the guidance of those in Colombia who were most affected. We attracted broad support across the church in the U.S. for a petition demanding justice for Tamarindo – not least because our close ties made these concerns extremely personal.

In April 2013, a community activist was murdered in his bed. IPC partners took accompaniers Sally Juarez and David Gifford to visit El Tamarindo, to share their condolences with the activist's grieving family. They arrived just as, without warning, bulldozers, police and paramilitaries started clearing a large tract of the community's land. Their photo documentation, coupled with strong support from allies in both Colombia and the U.S., convinced the Colombian government to declare the remaining land a protected "humanitarian zone" while the case was considered. Local IPC leaders Jairo Barriga and Germán Zárate started sending accompaniers (from the U.S. and Colombia) to spend time living alongside the community, sharing their struggles and their very simple living conditions. Just before Christmas in 2015, the local government supported a legal claim by big business and moved for final eviction. Accompaniers and local church partners were on the ground to back the community of El Tamarindo.

Shannan Vance-Ocampo, a Presbyterian pastor volunteering to coordinate Colombia advocacy work with the Presbyterian Peace Fellowship, contacted the U.S. Embassy immediately to ask for their support in stopping the eviction. PC(USA) mission co-worker Sarah Henken provided pastoral presence for the El Tamarindo community and updates for distant allies. A PC(USA) young-adult volunteer named Sophia Har helped develop a "solidarity with El Tamarindo" selfie campaign. Other human rights organizations in both Colombia and the U.S. began working all their lines of advocacy. The end result? The community's appeal to the Colombian Constitutional Court miraculously found its way to the top of their docket, and the Court ordered a stay of eviction until the company claiming the land provided the community with compensation, including title to alternative agricultural land, and funds to support their relocation and new start. Some in the community have been scattered with various financial offers or housing compensation, but despite community divisions, a core group has undertaken the daunting challenge of starting to build new homes and new farms all over again. There's still no sign of legally-required compensation from the government; the struggle continues.

Even in rare cases like El Tamarindo where the results of our "accompaniment" are visible, the results are mixed. Why do all of us engaged in the partnership continue? Why should the Presbyterian Peace Fellowship continue to lead this Colombia Accompaniment partnership, even as a peace agreement is being negotiated between the Colombian government and the FARC and ELN guerrillas? In large part, because the Presbyterian Church of Colombia continues to request it. They believe that the "post-accord" effort to build peace and re-integrate fighters is likely to present human rights organizations and communities like El Tamarindo with some of their greatest challenges to date. But we also continue because we have been transformed by the experience of accompanying the IPC. This is what it means to practice true mission in mutually-respectful partnership.

-LE/GZ

To the Edge of the Empire
Rick Ufford-Chase

Doris Rhoades died in March of 2016 at the age of 96, but when I visited her in 2014, she was still as sharp as ever. When I visited her at her home in Pilgrim Place – a retirement community for retired mission and church workers in Claremont California, she guided me as I drove us to a nearby Thai restaurant and then spent more than two hours regaling me with her life story. Doris was one of the wave of mission workers sent to China following the Second World War, and she served for six years before developing tuberculosis and being sent home to convalesce. After a few years back on her family's farm in Pennsylvania, she was sent overseas again – this time to work with displaced refugees in Hong Kong, where she stayed for over thirty years until she was in her sixties.

When she was called back to the United States this time, Doris went to work for the Presbyterian Mission program at the ecumenical church center in New York City. There she met and took up with a widower named Benton who had spent most of his career working in agricultural missions in South America. Doris told me stories of their courtship – long walks along the Hudson River on the Upper West Side – and how Benton proposed to her on the uptown bus one night as he accompanied her home from dinner at his apartment. I first met Benton and Doris when they were well into retirement. Though they were in their late 70's at that point, they were part of a group from Southern California who had come to the Arizona borderlands to learn more about the plight of economic migrants who were dying in the desert.

Benton and Doris have been my heroes in the faith, along with dozens of other mission workers I have known over the years. Together, these folks span many decades of service. They come out of Catholic orders like the Benedictines and Franciscans and Maryknoll, and from across the Protestant denominations. They represent great theological and vocational diversity, and they have served in locations all over the world. What they have in common is that their experience in mission has converted them to new understandings of their faith and the way that the U.S. is seen around the world. Their experience of accompanying partner churches through war and famine and economic desperation would be almost impossible for most of us here in the U.S. to imagine, and their unique worldview is critically important to the project of rethinking what it means to be church here in the heart of the Empire.

The mission workers who have most inspired me typically entered into mission with a great sense of call and conviction that the gospel impelled them to share good news, but they have themselves been converted by their experiences to a new understanding of the claim that the gospel makes in their own lives. What begins as a commitment to help others develops into a far deeper witness to solidarity and accompaniment with partner churches around the world that are struggling against the powers and principalities of our time: economic globalization, massive forced migrations, war, poverty, lack of access to good health-care and environmental devastation. In the process, sharing the good news of the gospel becomes a two-way street as our missionaries begin, as theologian Robert McAfee Brown put it, to "Read the Gospel with Third World Eyes."

That generation of mission workers who spanned the second half of the last century have also demonstrated a great capacity for reflecting on the missiological foundations of our work. Somehow they have managed simultaneously to confess the ways in which Christian mission has too often paved the way for colonization by Empire projects around the world, while recognizing and emulating the ways in which individual missionaries have stood up to the powers and principalities even during the worst of those moments. These mentors have inspired my own commitment to mission, pushing me to recognize that there is a great deal Christians have to atone for in the history of the mission movement. They have also shared the stories of courageous missionaries who have taken great risks for and with communities of people all over the world who have been on the underside of the Empire and the global economy. Both things are true. For many years I believed that my human rights and social justice work as a Presbyterian Mission worker on the U.S./Mexico border was on the outer fringe of the missionary movement, but it is clear to me now that I was tapping into a justice tradition of mission with very deep roots.

In my own Presbyterian tradition, we have a practice of doing this kind of careful self-accounting and rethinking our understanding of mission on a regular basis as the world changes around us. In the 1960's, Stony Point Center (where my wife and I today are Co-Directors) was home to an ecumenical partnership of seven Protestant denominations that intentionally did their training and orientation of outgoing mission workers together. I have met with many of those mission workers who were trained at Stony Point Center, and what is clear to me is that they were quite bold in their critique of the history of Protestant missions. After four months at Stony Point Center, mission workers left with a strong commitment to stand against the project of colonization and to stand with the global church wherever it was truly present with the people who were the targets of exploitation, violence and human rights abuses.

In the early 1990's, I was part of a group of some fifty young adults who came together to imagine new patterns of young adult mission service. We were clear that we wanted to create mission opportunities which would emphasize solidarity with the poor and oppressed. We hoped that those young adults would be converted in the process, and that they would develop and practice the concrete skills they would need to stand against Empire values for the rest of their lives. Looking back, I can see that we were part of a wave of similar critique that was taking place across denominational boundaries. Nearly thirty years later, there are young adult volunteer opportunities that reflect those values in many different Catholic and Protestant traditions.

Today, it seems clear to me that we must transform our understanding of mission once again. There are three primary areas in which I believe we need to recalibrate our understanding of mission to respond appropriately to the challenges of our time.

First, mission must be oriented toward confronting the significant systemic and structural expressions of sin that I have been wrestling with in this book. Here again I emphasize that I understand and have experienced the transformative power of the gospel in my own life, and have seen the power of the gospel to transform the lives of people in real ways – perhaps most obviously in the neighborhood Pentecostal and charismatic churches I have been blessed to visit in places like the Democratic Republic of the Congo and Mexico and Guatemala and Colombia and in immigrant communities in cities and small towns across the United States.

Having said that, I believe that every mission effort in our time must confront the evil of the "powers and principalities" that are destroying our world and our communities today: military-backed Empire-building projects, global corporations that consistently put short-term profit before our environment or our communities, systems of white supremacy that normalize the marginalization and the killing of black and brown people, and our acquiescence in the face of a gap between the world's rich and poor that perverts our deepest values and continually pushes our growing sense of insecurity and fear.

Elsa Tamez, one of my favorite theologians, speaks to a biblical translation problem that encourages our complacency here in the United States about the gospel imperative to address these fundamental challenges[1]:

> Before going ahead, it is important to clarify a problem of language. The Greek dikaiosyne tou theou is translated in all Spanish Bibles as 'the justice of God.' This is a much more ample term, enabling us to see dimensions that are not present in "the righteousness of God." The same is true for the Greek word adikia ('injustice'), which is often translated in English as 'wickedness.' These English translations lead one to think in a private and moral dimension, rather than in terms of social and political morality, as conceived in the Greek.

Tamez points out the ways in which our biblical translation has pushed us in subtle – and not so subtle – ways to emphasize a gospel of personal salvation at the expense of the gospel of liberation.

We do mission because we are commanded to share the good news, because it is a concrete expression of our task to construct the reign of God here on earth, and because it offers an opportunity for solidarity with the people Jesus cared for most. As I look at the history of Christian mission, when it is done poorly it quickly becomes captive to the worst abuses of power that Jesus stood against. When it is done well it becomes a lesson in humility and an

---

[1] Laurel Dykstra and Ched Myers, eds., *Liberating Biblical Study: Scholarship, Art, and Action in Honor of the Center and Library for the Bible and Social Justice* (Eugene, OR: Wipf & Stock Publishers, 2011), 175.

opportunity to show great courage as the church stands against those abuses. We should have no patience for mission that doesn't boldly confront the powers and principalities of our time.

> We should have no patience for mission that doesn't boldly confront the powers and principalities of our time.

The second adjustment needed in our mission practice is to continue to discern what we mean by "partnership." The Presbyterian Church (USA), here again mirroring similar commitments in our sister denominations, has spent the last three decades redesigning our mission efforts to embody our commitment to genuine partnership with sister churches around the world. This has been no easy task, given the paternalistic relationships to which all of us had grown accustomed over the previous century of missions. Approaching the task of mission as a shared responsibility with the churches we helped to plant in the 1800's is the right instinct, and in many places it has deepened our witness as we ourselves have been changed in the process. This is what I think God intends in every missional interaction, that the possibility of transformation exists for all parties involved.

The reality is that our historic mission efforts to plant churches also inculcated a sense of dependency in them that is pernicious and the natural result of the project of colonization. We need to work with our partner churches to "decolonize our mission." For us, this means giving up power and the assumption of privilege that we carry both explicitly and implicitly into most of our partner relationships. Many of our partners have recognized for a very long time that the financial support received from the church in the U.S. comes at a very high cost. Given the unequal distribution of resources in the world, breaking the dependency will take a sustained, concerted and faithful effort over many years to come.

There is a related and extremely challenging question in trying to transform our mission partnerships: What do we do when we disagree with our sister churches about fundamental matters of interpretation of scripture or exactly what our "mission" should be. For example, during the 1980's when the U.S. was funding the wars in Central America, and millions of refugees fled to come north to the United States, the refugees were at significant risk as they attempted to cross Mexico. The U.S. Government was paying the Mexican Government to interdict the refugees en route and send them back to Central America before they could reach the U.S. border. Corruption among police and military forces in Mexico was rampant, and stories of abuse committed against the Central Americans were ubiquitous. Unscrupulous smugglers formed brutal cartels that committed unspeakable acts of violence against an already traumatized population.

When church volunteers in the United States began setting up a route of safe houses to help high-risk refugees get safely across Mexico, we reached out to the Presbyterian Church in Mexico. For a wide variety of reasons that are too complex for discussion here, the church did not feel it was in a position to provide support for refugees (though there were a few courageous pastors who were notable exceptions to the rule). This presented a dilemma to Presbyterian mission workers like myself, working on the border. I had been through a mission orientation in which the mantra "we do mission in partnership" was ingrained in me, and I believed that was exactly where we should be. However, it was clear that my government's policies were putting Central Americans at risk at every step from the wars in their home countries to a highly dangerous journey north to a broken system of political asylum. In the end, we quietly sought out more natural allies among the poorest Catholic parishes that were the first places the Central Americans tended to seek refuge.

There is nothing easy about trying to manage the unhealthy power dynamics created over centuries of "colonized mission" efforts.

Many of our partner churches around the world confront the same temptation to submit to the powers and principalities that we face here in the United States, but in many cases the cost of resistance is potentially far higher for them than it is for us. This means that it is often easier for us to call out the forces of domination in their countries than it is for them to do so. Conversely, I would note that some of our partners have noticed our reticence to name injustice or take a prophetic stand in our own country where the cost to us may be higher. Though it is very challenging, we should be cultivating relationships of confidence like the one Linda Eastwood describes between the Presbyterian Church of Colombia and the Presbyterian Church and Presbyterian Peace Fellowship in the United States. As we have worked to support the Presbyterian Church of Colombia in moments of crisis, it has not been unusual for us to receive mixed messages – "yes we want to denounce this abuse publicly." "No the timing is not right." This speaks to a situation of high risk, and being able to listen carefully to our partners and respond with care is critically important. We know one another well, we respect one another, and we trust one another.

One more note about the challenges of "partnership" in our missiological relationships today. What do we do when our historic partner churches don't share our theological commitments, or we don't share theirs? This has become a significant issue in my own denomination in the last few years as we in the Presbyterian Church (USA) have made changes to our constitution to remove or edit the specific portions that would deny the possibility of ordination for leadership and marriage to all people who are in open, non-heterosexual relationships. We are not alone in the pressure that we have felt from global partners who are deeply convinced that this decision was in error. In fact, if anything, the divisions are more intense in the Episcopal and Methodist traditions where they are one global church as opposed to our situation of being a U.S. church with global partners. Numerous historical church partners from around the world have formally broken off relations and asked our mission workers to leave, which has been a deeply painful experience for us and, I expect, for them as well.

When this happens, it seems to me that we must allow for gracious difference of opinion. When those churches want to remain in relationship with us, I am in favor of continuing our work together so long as both parties can do so without violating their own conscience. We must be open about our differences, clear about who we are, transparent (and prepared to be repentant) about the inherent and unhealthy power dynamics that exist between us, and respectful of one another – even when we may be uncomfortable. For instance, many of our partner churches choose not to ordain women. While I am not in agreement that women should not be permitted to provide leadership in the church, I don't feel it is my place to attempt to change their practice. The stronger the partnership, the greater the possibility for open and respectful dialogue with one another about our differences.

It is no more "equal" to give up our own voice in the face of disagreement from a partner church than it is to insist on having our own way and dictating the terms of the agreement. The alternative is to strive for partnerships like the Colombia Accompaniment Project. This works best when we are in partnership with churches that are willing to hear our voice as we hear theirs, and to play to our strengths as we play to theirs. In the end, partnership must mean respecting one another as equals and then seeking common ground that asks neither partner to give up core principles or convictions.

The third assumption about how our understanding and practice of mission must change is that mission must be affordable. Like our local congregations, regional organizations, theological institutions, and national church structures, our mission efforts have fallen prey to the seductions of dominant culture values. The result is the demoralization of a church that has long prided itself on mission in and to the world. Efforts to suggest that we must simply give more money to the work of mission are well meaning, but they miss the underlying problem. We can't afford a professional class of missionaries that is led to believe that we will be able to support them and their families without a dramatic shift in our understanding of the call of mission and church work.

I believe we absolutely need a corps of long-term mission workers who form the bridge for those "partnerships among equals" that I've described. The problem is not that we don't need people to serve as those bridges, it's that we will need to find new ways to sustain those who have felt such a call. We need to throw out our understanding of compensation that we have carefully crafted over the last sixty years, and instead move toward a system based on demonstrated need. I would make this same case for our pastors, our theologians, and our governing body staff, and I believe that our mission personnel are uniquely positioned to lead the way.

Here are a few thoughts about what that might look like:

- We should resurrect the old "Mission Diaconal" pattern of service, in which the mission worker and his or her family make a commitment to live at roughly the same standard of living as the people with whom they are working in the partner country. This should be our primary pattern of service, and Diaconal Workers should be permitted to continue in that pattern of service for as many years as they feel called to do so, and can sustain it.

- The mission diaconal pattern should be flexible and based on an appreciation of the different kinds of financial need that we typically face in different stages of life. Though I lived on a modest stipend for the first fifteen years of my career, I have needed significantly more income during the last ten years as I have raised three children through their teenage years. I expect that things will shift back again as my kids are able to take responsibility for themselves. Sometimes the needs of our church workers may exceed the ability of the community to support them. When that happens, we need relationships of trust in which we can encourage healthy decisions for both the individual and the community. This kind of service is not for everyone.

- We should ask our partner churches to help us make this pattern of service sustainable by working with us to provide appropriate housing similar to what they would expect for local pastors or church members. Wherever possible, we should look at the possibility of creating intentional communities where we can live more simply, and support one another in avoiding the pitfalls of dominant culture consumerism. I'm not suggesting that we resurrect the old "mission compounds" here, but instead that we create small intentional communities that could easily include members of our partner churches or local colleagues themselves. This makes sense relationally, it makes sense theologically, and it makes sense financially.

- We should ask our church-related universities to help us figure out how to make education for the children of missionaries or church workers available at a modest expense, so that those called to church service do not need to go into debt for their children to receive a decent education, nor give up their commitment to a modest standard of living.

- We need to rethink retirement entirely. Currently, most denominations in the United States assume that we must pay a salary with a pension benefit that will allow our church workers to retire independently in a system that has grown to be extremely expensive here in the United States. We need new, much less expensive alternatives. What if we transformed old manses and churches into multigenerational living situations that have as part of their mission the care for retired church workers? Or what about this? The PC(USA) still has well over one hundred camp and conference centers and there are similar facilities belonging to other denominations all over our nation. What if we were building affordable living arrangements on those campuses as alternative retirement communities? We have so many more resources than we recognize we have.

- We need to beef up our young adult mission patterns that are creating a new generation of folks who will live these counter-Empire values all their lives, and we need to recognize that their year of mission service is far more about orienting them to a lifetime of commitment and service and resistance than it is about the communities to whom they offer a year or two of service. This is work to which many of our denominations have already made a significant commitment, though in my experience it needs to be given far greater priority in our overall mission strategy.

- We need to put far more energy into the creation of a pattern of mission service that will take advantage of the passion of retired, older adults who want to serve. We should make it easy for an older adult to step into mission service that is fully engaging. If we can pull this off, everyone wins.

- Mission workers need to be much more connected to their local, sending congregations. Mission workers should go out not just because they feel a personal sense of call, but because that call has been tested and honed in a community or a congregation that believes in the call as well and is able to help pay for it. Many of the traditional Protestant denominations have raised money for missions through a unified budget, effectively cutting off the relationship between mission workers and their sponsoring congregations. By and large, unified giving is an experiment that ultimately has failed, and the reasons are obvious. People are transformed by relationships. They give to things that they believe in, and what they believe in is someone whom they know personally and who is doing work to which they are committed.

- Hierarchy will need to be flattened out to keep up with the speed and the ease of communications with the internet. Having said that, there will always be a need for coordination in our efforts, and an orientation toward our values and commitments as we do this work together. Presbyterians have been trying to do this, with some success, through the formation of Mission Networks, in which communities who share a concern in a particular country communicate regularly with one another and with church and community leaders from that same country.

- We need to continue to build on the important work we have already done to make mission bi-directional. Given our position as a church in the heart of Empire, no one needs conversion more than we do in the United States, and no one is better prepared to offer us wisdom and guidance than our partners from around the world who understand the sinfulness of the militarized, globalized, extractionist economy because they have been the victims of it. Here too, we must offer to bring mission workers into our own homes, share our vehicles and other resources, and nurture strong faith communities together, both because as an act of faithfulness and because it's the smartest way to pay for it.

I confess that I have lived these values and solutions better at some moments in my life than I have in others. My wife and I have chosen to create and live in communities of this sort for twenty-four out of our twenty-five-year marriage, but we find ourselves caught up in dominant cultural expectations and values just like everyone else. The challenge to our church is to have the courage to admit that our current practice is simply unsustainable, and then do all we can to support efforts to create communities that will help us resist these cultural expectations, and be more faithful together. As a class of people, mission workers have shown perhaps the greatest courage across the history of our church, and I would like to see them lead the whole church to the edge of the Empire.

Here's another bit of wisdom from John Fife, my pastor of twenty years from the Arizona borderlands, and Alison Harrington's predecessor at Southside Presbyterian Church. I used to argue with John about how desperate the world situation is, and how unprepared the church is to meet the challenge. His response was thought-provoking, and for me – compelling: "Show me another institution that has a presence in every country and nearly every community around the world, and that has as its core tenets principles of justice and peace, and I'm in. I think the church is the best shot we've got."

I'm with John. This is the moment to create a new, sustainable pattern of Christian mission that can lead all of us into new, healthy partnerships that have the potential to respond to the real challenges confronting us today. When I think about this set of opportunities, I can literally feel my pulse begin to quicken.

Discussion Questions:

1. What experience have you had with mission? What do you think Rick means by our need to "decolonize our mission?" Can you give an example?

2. The Presbyterian Peace Fellowship has archived dispatches from the Colombia Accompaniers over the last decade. You can find them at http://presbypeacefellowship.org/newsletter/colombia_report Ask each person to find a favorite report and talk about what our accompaniers have been learning and experiencing in this remarkable partnership.

3. What do you think of John Fife's belief that the church is uniquely positioned as a grassroots institution that has a worldwide network, making it the most effective place from which to organize to resist injustice?

4. Rick has suggested some significant changes in how we think about compensation for mission workers, then pushed further to suggest that mission workers should be leading the way for the broader church to reconsider how we sustain our leaders financially. Do you think he gets it right? Why or why not?

Chapter 9
Institutional Church as an Expression of Solidarity

Beyond Connectionalism
Aric Clark

Much of how we think of life in the American Christian denominations is based on a foundation of connectional relationships. However, as we imagine the church as it could be, as it needs to become, connectionalism isn't sufficient. We need a sturdier virtue upon which to build our common identity.

American Protestant Christianity relies on voluntary association. The fact that American society (rightfully!) rejected the establishment of any particular religion, combined with our individualistic culture means that as a Christian one can identify as Presbyterian, or Methodist, or Baptist, or Pentecostal, or Seventh Day Adventist, or none-of-the-above and no one can stop you. Not to mention other religious, or non-religious affiliations. As a result, denominational loyalty tends to be pretty weak. Many people shift religious affiliations several times over their lifetime. This is not a new thing, but it's a trend that is only increasing.

To push against this trend, mainline Christians often talk about the virtue of "connectionalism." Connectionalism, simply, is the conviction that we're better together than apart. Typically, we invoke connectionalism to encourage participation in, and support of, institutional religious structures – Synods, Conferences, Districts, Regions, or Presbyteries. We often sell connectionalism as a good unto itself, or an accomplished fact ("this denomination is a *connectional* denomination"). When we make an argument for the value of connectionalism, we usually base that argument on a trust in the superior wisdom of the group through a diversity of experiences and perspectives.

Plainly, connectionalism has failed. This is apparent in the rapid dissolution of denominational distinctiveness. To many of us it is made even more obvious by the exposure of so many church institutional structures as the last gasps of Christendom. As Christian practice moves further and further from the mainstream it is becoming clear that many of our organizations were structured so that they were dependent upon, and even encouraging of, western Christian hegemony. Maintaining connections isn't a good reason for sustaining institutions mired in systemic oppression.

Furthermore, we live in a world where connection is easier than ever. I scroll through thousands of people's daily experiences and opinions each night before bed and wake up to fresh notifications from friends, family and strangers every morning. I'm connected to people in greater numbers, with more intimacy, and in greater diversity than the architects of church polity likely imagined. Compared to the modes of connection that the internet and personal electronics offer us, as well as the cultural innovations that have arisen in that context, the structures of the church are hopelessly obtuse.

As we look to form communities which will thrive in our already highly interconnected, post-Christendom era, we can't and we shouldn't depend on connectionalism to guide us. We need a more robust virtue to assist both in developing cohesion, and in instilling a sense of direction. Instead of connectionalism we should begin to speak of *solidarity*.

Solidarity demands more from us. Connectionalism requires only that I be, well, connected to you. Social media demonstrates how low a bar this really is. We can be connected, even tightly, without sharing much mutual affection or common purpose. Solidarity, by contrast, requires that I actively identify with you (or work to do so), that I stand with you in a way which is personally risky. Solidarity is a more thoroughly Christian virtue.

Solidarity has a trajectory. The only goal of connectionalism is to get, and then stay, connected. Solidarity implies resistance to oppression and injustice. Solidarity requires that I not only identify with you, but that I work *for* you. The focus of connectionalism is membership. The focus of solidarity is liberation.

Solidarity draws us out of ourselves. Connectionalism draws us into ourselves. While connectionalism asks those who are already in the room to turn toward each other, solidarity encourages us to turn as a group toward those who have been historically marginalized and excluded. Connectionalism is concerned with representation because that is "only fair." Solidarity

> **Solidarity draws us out of ourselves. Connectionalism draws us into ourselves.**

seeks something that is more than "only fair." A church based in solidarity knows that she doesn't exist for herself, but for the sake of the world.

Even committed, faithful church goers often have difficulty understanding the purpose or nature of regional and national church structures. Ask your average congregant why the bishop, or the presbytery, or region, functions the way it does and you may get blank stares. Solidarity provides better answers for both the why and the how of church organization.

So why are we joined with all these other Christians? Why is the church more than just my local congregation, indeed, why is it past time for us to be drawn out of our denominational silos as well?

Because we need to struggle on their behalf, and we need them to struggle on our behalf in order to be fully Christian. Because the struggle is too big for us alone. Because justice hasn't been fully realized. Because God's peace hasn't been made fully manifest. In short, because we still have work to do.

How shall we be joined with all these other Christians?

We must learn to place the marginalized and oppressed before ourselves. Just as the church must give herself for the sake of the world, so within the church the powerful must give themselves for the sake of the powerless. Beyond seeking to be merely representational, we must disproportionately lift into leadership members of the oppressed groups with whom we aim to stand in solidarity.

Inequalities of status and opportunity, whether based on race, gender, sexual identity, or economic class, must continually be exposed and demolished. Resistance to injustice must become a mode of operation, a spiritual discipline continually practiced inwardly and outwardly. We must cultivate habits and structures designed to make room for frequent calls to repentance. Among other things, this means training ourselves to seek out and listen to criticism coming from the margins.

Finally, we must be joined with other Christians in continually evolving ways as we refuse to allow the support systems to ever take precedence over the struggle itself. Living in solidarity with the oppressed must become our guide, and the particular ways and means will adjust accordingly. We must resist the idolatry of becoming a church that is the same today, tomorrow, and forever, and instead be the church which is living toward a peace which passes understanding.

-AC

There Is No Fear In Love
Rick Ufford-Chase

The fourth chapter of 1 John provides theological language for Aric's exhortation to adopt solidarity as the guiding principle of our institutions:

> *God is Love, and those who abide in love, abide in God, and God abides in them. Love has been perfected among us in this: that we may have boldness on the day of judgment, for as God is, so are we in this world. There is no fear in love, but perfect love casts out fear; for fear has to do with punishment, and whoever fears has not reached perfection in love. We love because God first loved us. Those who say, "I love God," and hate their brothers or sisters, are liars; for those who do not love a brother or sister whom they have seen, cannot love God whom they have not seen. The commandment we have from God is this: those who love God must love their brothers and sisters also. (1 John 4:16b-21, NRSV)*

Fear is the overarching characteristic of the broader culture in the United States today. Look just below the belligerence and bravado of our politicians, and it is easy to intuit the deep sense of insecurity in the general population to which they are responding. We feel unsafe about our livelihoods. Many of us feel alienated and disconnected from our neighbors. We are concerned that our kids won't be able to find secure jobs to care for their families. Too many of us are just a medical crisis away from economic disaster. Many of us are trying to juggle the responsibilities of our own families with the livelihoods of others who work for us in small businesses that never quite make it to economic stability.

As citizens, we are anxious about the constant state of a war on terror to which our country has committed itself, fearful as terrorist attacks are replayed endlessly in the media. Our fear of anyone – and perhaps everyone – who is "different" from us is intentionally fueled by public discourse that suggests building walls on our borders, patrolling our neighborhoods, arming ourselves to "stand our ground," locking up criminals, and refusing entry to all we see as enemies (currently, Muslims). Our growing fear is not accidental – it is the result of a well-funded and ceaseless campaign by the powers and principalities that stand to gain big while our anxiety grows, as we buy into the myth that redemptive violence can make us safer.

This text from the book of 1 John is a message to all Christians about the only appropriate response to our fear: "Perfect love casts out fear, and those who say that they love God but cannot love their sister or brother – are liars." Love, the way it is used in this passage, is what Aric describes as solidarity. Solidarity is, when rightly performed, the most visible indication of our seriousness of intention to love all of our sisters and brothers fully and radically.

Just as it pushes us beyond fear of the "other," this passage also holds us accountable to a far higher standard in our relationships with one another within the church as well. We are called to something much more profound than connectionalism. The text insists that we must stick with one another, learn from one another, challenge and change one another, and strengthen one another in our shared witness. We must model this kind of love within our church if we are to have any hope whatsoever of holding up its value to the rest of the world.

This is why Facebook and Twitter and any other kind of social media we are likely to come up with, I believe, can never be a replacement for being in face-to-face relationships with one another. Despite the many possibilities offered by social media, it is not designed to help me engage with people who are likely to disagree with me. It is entirely possible to spend all of my time surrounding myself with literally thousands of other people who look at the world much in the same way I do. Social media can often feel like an echo chamber in which like-minded people share their common experiences and perceptions, both positive and negative. No one appears to be safe from this tendency. Whether we tend liberal or conservative, the likelihood that we will lose the ability to engage in thoughtful, civil, theologically-grounded discourse with one another is extremely high.

Social media and the internet are useful tools to keep us connected to one another, and even to draw us into awareness of injustice or activism experienced by sisters and brothers around the world, but while this medium can supplement our relational solidarity, it can never take the place of connecting us to one another in the deeper acts of solidarity to which God is calling us. In my judgment, congregations and worshiping communities that are isolated unto themselves, and have no intentional mechanism for joining with others to address the big questions of systemic oppression or destruction of the environment, are at a significant disadvantage when it comes doing the work of solidarity.

For Christians to claim a moral voice in our highly pluralistic context, we must have habits of discerning and developing our collective voice, and offering our shared witness. That ability is among the most important attributes of our denominational structures in the Protestant tradition, which have developed highly sophisticated ways of helping us to offer a unified witness to the world. So while I agree with Aric that connectionalism is not a value in and of itself, I do believe very strongly in the importance of finding ways to connect with one another to take on the work of solidarity. I am concerned, however, that we have forgotten the reason we are called to be in relationship with one another in the first place, and that we have over-professionalized the relatively simple act of association.

Here's the problem: we are practiced at identifying, nurturing and affirming leaders who know how to build up and protect the institution of the church. These are legitimate and important skills, but they are the wrong skills for the church at this moment in time. We need to emphasize an entirely different set of skills to carry us into a new way of being church in our time. This will be extremely challenging because there is no such thing as a "one size fits all" approach in the complex landscape in which we are called to do ministry today.

At the local level, our pastors and lay leaders must develop the ability to simultaneously: 1) listen to the deepest desires of the congregants, 2) read the "signs of the times" in the broader culture, and 3) interpret scripture to guide the community through these turbulent times. Doing all three of these things well will allow us to craft a new kind of consensus about what kind of faith communities we will be. It will offer guidance and reassurance as our congregations and faith communities discern a way forward. This kind of leadership involves a skill set that must be intentionally developed.

Leaders who focus on only one of these three tasks to the exclusion of the other two doom the community to failure. A focus only on listening to the needs of those already within the faith community typically breeds complacency and irrelevance. To focus only on the "signs of the times" in the world around us runs the risk that we will become political panderers (whether we lean left or right). A focus only on scripture to the exclusion of an appreciation for the challenges posed by the dominant culture leads quickly to fundamentalism that misses God's actual love for, and engagement in, a complex world. These skills must be developed in our pastors, and the lay leaders in our congregations should be required to develop and demonstrate competence in all three of these areas as well: learning active listening skills, developing an unwavering commitment to acts of solidarity and mission that stretch the community, and becoming confident with a variety of lenses through which to interpret scripture.

These are the marks of leadership that will encourage strong faith communities, but there is a greater challenge if we are to embrace the bold and effective commitment to solidarity that Aric challenges us to imagine together. Congregationalism tends too often, at least in the U.S., to manifest primarily as isolated communities that don't have the skills to fully engage the world around them. And connectionalism is primarily oriented toward the maintenance of the dominant culture, Empire values that we are called to resist because we are the people of God. On the other hand, the call to demonstrate solidarity is a value that is tailor-made for the anti-Empire, anti-racist, watershed-connected, nonviolence-seeking, genuinely inclusive church of our time.

Synods and presbyteries and conferences and dioceses and classis and districts: these "associations" provide the opportunity to move us from acts of charity to acts of solidarity. They ensure that we will be known for what we believe and what we do together. They force us to test our ideas with one another, to learn from one another, and to seek boldness together. For many decades, most of our denominations have fallen far short of this vision. Instead, in far too many instances, we have been preoccupied with institutional preservation.

In such a context, especially when we feel the institution we love is at risk, we typically become fixated on defending our theological purity, and assuring that anyone who goes off message is brought back into line. We trust one another less and less, and we place ever-greater strictures on one another's freedom to live into creative and daring expressions of gospel commitment. In my experience within the Presbyterian Church (USA), we have worked out our anxieties and lack of trust by layering on more and more rules designed to ensure the protection of our theological convictions in the institution, and we find our regional meetings consumed by the judicial necessity to keep one another in line.

It's no wonder that the wrist-slapping and gate-keeping functions have soured many of us on the act of being in relationship with one another. In the last few years, Presbyterians have begun taking steps to address this reality by dramatically streamlining the "Book of Order" which governs our interactions, trying to put the responsibility for our relationships back in our local presbyteries. This is good news, and it offers hope that the institution we created is capable of monitoring itself. But we've only begun to scratch the surface of this problem, and my colleagues in other denominations tell me they confront similar challenges. Most of our denominations remain caught up in the infighting and bickering that inspires no one I know to become a part of us. And the non-denominational expressions of Christian community in the United States have their own problems. Those problems are less about organizational structures, but it seems clear to me that many of our evangelical sisters and brothers are encountering challenges as they try to agree on what they will emphasize as the heart of the gospel message. This is made far more difficult by the skepticism in our broader culture about the hypocrisy many believe to be the constant condition of the Christian Church.

So what would it look like to claim a sense of excitement for the work of solidarity? How can we re-energize and develop substance in our collective effort to claim our moral and prophetic voice from our position in the heart of the Empire?

We need to find new ways to be in association with one another.

Worship should be at the center of our collective life. If we haven't done so already, our regional bodies should lay down the mind-numbing work of endless committee meetings and reports that are throwbacks to a different era. Instead, our time should focus on creating opportunities for thoughtful engagement with one another about the challenges laid out in this book. If we embrace our call as followers of Jesus, our regional and national bodies will err on the side of taking risks on behalf of a radical gospel that calls us into direct engagement with the most troubling issues in the world around us.

Within those regional associations, building meaningful relationships with one another should offer room for both passion and passionate disagreement as we strive together to engage the work of solidarity and love – the hard love as described in 1 John. The goal of our discourse must not be to prove the superiority of our position over an opponent, but instead to seek a common understanding of God's will for our shared witness.

This is almost impossible for most of us to imagine at this point. We have lost the ability to cultivate "courageous space" where we can speak and hear hard truths with one another. Many of us have spoken for years of "safe space," but my friends who do not share my unearned privilege have helped me to understand that, too often, my call for "safe space" ends up meaning that no one is allowed to question my sense of entitlement.

Instead, we must strive to create a place where our dialogue is open, honest and respectful – "courageous conversations." Though I often find myself challenged in these conversations, I've learned that if I can summon the courage to listen non-defensively, I invariably come away from the conversation with deeper relationships and far greater understanding. As sure as I am about the rightness of my understanding of scripture and my experience of God, I am equally humble in my awareness that for fifty-two years I have been a continual work in progress. The

> The things I know to be true today are quite likely to be challenged and changed tomorrow.

things I know to be true today are quite likely to be challenged and changed tomorrow. That's why I believe in community, and it's why I am firmly committed to "being church" with people who see the world differently than I do. For those of us in the Reformed traditions, holding onto core values while allowing for the possibility of radical change in ourselves is a hallmark of who we are as the people of God.

Some would have us believe that the wiser course of action in this difficult time is actually to avoid taking on difficult and controversial topics. This is problematic both because it ignores the radical nature of Jesus' witness in his own time, and because it will lead to a witness so tepid as to be meaningless in our own. Now is the time to redefine what it means to be Christian community and to commit together to wrestle with tough issues.

We must invite those who reside on the margins of our communities to find in us the place where their voices will be honored, even when it makes the traditionalists among us anxious.

The art form, for me and for many of us, is to share our understanding of the claim the gospel makes on our lives with both the greatest humility and the greatest boldness that we can muster. Our organizational structures should encourage nuanced discourse and relationships of confidence, though there is nothing easy about what I am proposing. I expect it will grow more difficult as we seek to craft a shared consensus with more and more people who represent far greater diversity than we have encountered thus far. White people, accustomed to setting the terms of what it means to be church for so long, will have to find ways to accept the fact that ours is no longer the defining cultural reality.

Our first act must be to welcome all who feel a nudging or a call to give their lives over to God. I think Pope Francis gets this exactly right: the question is not whom would God condemn (since, after all, our scripture makes it clear that this is not our judgment to make), but instead, who does God choose to love? In the emerging communities of faith that commit to the project of solidarity, we will be defined by our willingness to include and be transformed by the people who make us most anxious – the generation who describe themselves as "spiritual but not religious," those who have been deeply wounded by their experience of exclusion from the institution of church, as well as the folks who show up at Black Lives Matter demonstrations, or stand with the displaced people of El Tamarindo in Colombia, or with migrants like Rosa at Southside Presbyterian Church in Tucson, or with Syrian refugees or those who have been incarcerated. In short, we're talking about the people who make many in our society feel most afraid.

In a church committed to solidarity the question is, "Where we will choose to make our stand?" If we are afraid of the powers and the principalities of the Empire, or if we are afraid of losing our "respectability", it's going to be tough to make the case that our lives have, in fact, been transformed by the love of God and the life, death and resurrection of Jesus, the Christ. Moderation, long-held as a central value in the church in the heart of Empire, is going to have to be abandoned as we embrace the church and the witness of boldness as Jesus envisioned.

The Synod of the Northeast of the Presbyterian Church (USA) is an interesting case study in what it looks like for a mid-level church body to try to redefine itself in these ways. When I arrived in the Hudson Valley of New York in 2008, Stony Point Center was the host for the annual gathering of the Synod Assembly. Each of 23 Presbyteries would send representatives – pastors and lay people – for an annual assembly that lasted a day and a half. I attended my first several meetings as an observer, and could see no point in the entire exercise.

There was little sense of Spirit, and the primary purpose of the gathering appeared to be to assure that recalcitrant or wayward presbyteries were appropriately reigned in and held accountable to the institution of the PC(USA). If there was a genuine sense of connection or enthusiasm from the local congregations represented by the presbytery commissioners, I couldn't feel it. There was an active debate going on in the hallways, and in front of the coffee maker in the dining room, regarding whether it was time to simply let the Synod die, and had I been asked to weigh in on the matter, that's the direction my vote would have gone.

But then, something happened. There was an intentional move to recruit younger people into positions of leadership and to ask for – and value – their opinions. A steering team made a genuine, and largely successful, effort to listen to stakeholders across the Synod, which includes all of New England, New York and New Jersey. There was a spirit that moved traditionalists who had cared for the life and work of the Synod for decades to open themselves up to new ways of understanding our work together. Slowly, we discerned a shared commitment to strengthen our reformed witness in a context that is overwhelmingly secular and extremely religiously pluralistic. In short, a few thoughtful leaders who understood the art of crafting consensus began to help us to find a new way forward.

What would happen, key stakeholders wondered, if we understood our work to be not the creation of programs (which we can't afford to staff, and which don't engage the people in our communities in any significant way), but instead to build relationships of confidence with one another with the express purpose of articulating our shared witness around the most compelling social issues of our day? A consensus emerged that we could actually be the vanguard for the national church, seeking to witness to a new way of being church in a secular cultural context that is likely to be increasingly evident across the country over the coming decade – even in the places where Christendom still reigns at the moment.

Several years later, our deeper relationships across the Synod are helping us to develop the capacity to reflect together about the challenges of Empire and entrenched racism. Together, we are taking on issues like gun violence, supporting people who have been incarcerated, and connection those who are concerned about fossil fuel extraction. Increasingly, we are dealing with matters of genuine substance, and we are doing it in powerful ways because we have laid claim to the work of solidarity together. So far, this has been about drawing people together around their shared passions and encouraging a thoughtful self-inventory about what it means to be church, eschewing the historic model of creating programs and hiring staff to take on the challenges directly.

In an example of our ability to sustain a far deeper conversation, the question of dealing with racism, the question of dealing with racism and the challenge to "decolonize" our faith became far more real in the context of the synod's relationship with Witherspoon Presbyterian Church in Princeton, NJ. This historically African-American church was founded in 1879 by a former slave named William Robeson (father of the famed singer and civil rights activist Paul Robeson). In 1901, after twenty-one years of service, the Presbytery forced Rev. Robeson out of the church because of his effort to combat Jim Crow laws in Princeton. The congregation fell on hard financial times and was forced to sell its manse.

In 2015, the Synod made the decision to forgive a $175,000 loan it had made to the church to repurchase the manse and renovate the church. This was an intentional act of reconciliation and reparation, initiated and accompanied by a formal apology by New Brunswick Presbytery, and it is exactly the kind of behavior the church is called to model.

I suspect that such opportunities abound across our church. What if our regional and national bodies committed to an honest effort to atone for the ways in which our institutions have been built on land stolen from Native Americans, and with resources built on the slave economy? What if, as we sell our churches and other properties in the process of downsizing and re-creating ourselves, we offered

178 \ Faithful Resistance

concrete reparations for the immeasurable economic harm (to say nothing of the spiritual or emotional harm) we have done to Native Americans, to African-Americans, to Mexican-Americans or other people of color, to women and to queer folks? Though I expect such a prospect sounds exhausting to many in our predominantly white churches, the experience here in the Synod of the Northeast has been that such acts are freeing us to be the new church we are called to be. I expect that we would gain respect among sisters and brothers who have been historically marginalized in our churches, and we cannot even imagine where that respect might lead us.

I get excited when I imagine regional and national bodies of Christians not as an exercise of obligation, or a place to fight with one another, but instead as voluntary associations that enliven us because of the transformative work we are called to do together. I imagine them not as budgets that we strain to maintain, but instead as lean, inexpensive gatherings that actually help us to be in solidarity with one another in our own communities and around the world. My own presbytery has helped me to understand that our gathering could be not just another boring meeting but, instead, an opportunity to form much deeper relationships of confidence that propel us into the world, offering a bold and compelling witness to the claim that Jesus has made in our lives.

I have heard Alison Harrington say that the work Southside Church is doing to support undocumented people in their community cannot be done in isolation. It depends upon relationships of trust with colleagues across the church, and a clear indication that we are all in this together. As Jin, Laura, John and the students of the first cohort of Underground Seminary are living into their marvelous experiment, their work will be immeasurably strengthened if we all join with them to create vibrant communities of resistance. What Linda Eastwood and Germán Zárate and the U.S. accompaniers are doing together with members of the Presbyterian Church of Colombia cannot be successful without a strong, committed community of churches that are willing to do the advocacy work necessary to protect the people of Tamarindo.

Individually, our communities can offer resistance. Together, we can transform the world. Solidarity works for me.

-RUC

Discussion Questions:

1. What do you think about Aric's assertion that connectionalism draws our focus inward, while solidarity pushes us outward? Can you share specific examples of ways in which you have experienced both?

2. Think of a time when you have been excited to be a part of an exciting social movement? What was it that energized you?

3. What do you think Rick means by "crafting consensus?"

4. What do you think of the distinction between "safe space" and "courageous space?" Have you had a group experience where there was permission to challenge one another in ways that were respectful, but true to each person's experience? What did it feel like?

Chapter 10
Dismantling the Corporate Church as a Step Toward Liberation

This chapter offers a critique that is specific to the Presbyterian Church (USA), and offers suggestions to take on the challenges that are uniquely ours. However, most of our sister denominations in the Protestant tradition have experienced similar pressures and responded to those pressures in similar ways. I expect that much of what J. Herbert Nelson and I are wrestling with would find currency in those other traditions as well.

A New Way Forward
J. Herbert Nelson

We face a critical challenge in difficult times as members of the Presbyterian Church (USA). Over the years we have lived in denial regarding the evident decline in the life of our denomination. Our decline is often measured by decreasing membership, but there are more factors that must be considered. We are diminished in our spiritual witness to a world in need of hearing Jesus' words of hope and healing. We are broken by our internal and personal need for power and privilege. We are blinded from seeing the truth about ourselves both individually and collectively due to our negative critiques of one another. Our self-serving categories of liberal, moderate and conservative have divided us into political descriptions that have no place in the Church of Jesus Christ. In short, we've looked too much at our desires for control and not enough at Jesus' love. Thus we find ourselves in a time when recalibration of our efforts to know Jesus is vitally important to our future as a denomination.

Since the reunion of the Northern and Southern Presbyterian Denominations in 1983, we've fought an internal civil war over the issues of evangelism, social justice commitments, polity, theological reform, financial matters, racial and gender justice, full inclusion of lesbian and gay persons, ending the occupation of Palestinians, and many more matters of concern. It seems as though we reunited as two totally different denominations and then decided to work out the details after doing so. We are now facing the fallout as this thirty-three-year experience is grinding to an apparent end. Despite a remnant of dissent, it appears that the worst of the internal storm is over and the damage assessment is in process. Beyond the damage assessment must be a sense of the way forward. Where does the immediate rebuilding of a viable future begin in the PC(USA)? This challenge faces us as we mourn the loss of congregations, friends in the pews, institutions' money and familiar structure.

I am reminded of the disciples in the Upper Room at Mary's house, fasting for forty days and forty nights trying to hear from the Holy Spirit to find their way forward after the crucifixion of Jesus. The Apostles of the Lord were brought to a significant moment to tarry with the Holy Spirit and seek direction for the way ahead. The future of the Church rested on their ability to commune with one another and reach one accord through their faith. Yes, we are there now. What a fellowship! What a joy divine! Leaning on the everlasting arm! We are dependent on the one who has all power to bring us from gall to glory! I write to offer some specific foci that will get us started on this journey to rethinking our way ahead.

1. **Reclaiming Prayer, Biblical Literacy, Fervent Worship and Theological Discourse As Celebration**

   Our spiritual formation must be the source of our guidance in the days ahead. Fasting, prayer, discernment, and implementation require a sense of intense spiritual focus. Both clergy and lay leadership must submit themselves to the leading of the Holy Spirit while issuing the call to the entire Church to do likewise. We must be led into a posture of submission to the Holy Spirit. We already know what happens when we take over and believe that the Church belongs to us. This is the basis of our dilemma now. The moment we feel we can succeed and attain victory over sin by the strength of our will alone is the moment we are worshipping the will. We are challenged to reclaim the Sovereignty of God as our mantra through submission to the Holy Spirit. This is more than intellectual posturing. We must have fervor emanating from our hearts when we teach, preach, pray, and worship while demonstrating and sharing the love of Jesus.

2. **Our Theology Must Be Made Understandable to the Un-churched Without Dumbing Down its Content**

   Presbyterians are noted for depth-filled theology. We must continue to produce credible theology that makes persons think and feel the power of the Gospel. Our challenge is to produce theological materials for the marginalized as our mission field in the United States is growing. The poor and marginalized must not only read theological materials about them, but also designed for them to receive the instruction, guidance and spiritual counsel needed to engage their daily lives while becoming partners in their own liberation. Pastors, Christian Educators, scholars and other writers are challenged to recognize that our future as a denomination will be dependent on evangelizing and preparing persons from different socio-economic strata, literacy levels, experiences of oppressions, religious influences and national/international origins.

3. Deeper Commitments to Ecumenical/Interfaith Conversations and Actions

Presbyterians have cultivated relationships with ecumenical and interfaith partners throughout our history. We are joined biblically with both Judaism and Islam through Abraham. It is important that we emphasize the collective power of uniting various faith expressions through our continued participation in ecumenical and interfaith relations. Disagreement on issues should not de-emphasize the power of these alliances in the future work of the PC(USA). We must be willing to stay at the table while calling one another into accountability, because we are stronger together. Our challenge is to find common spaces to build hope in the world. Our way forward will largely be determined as to how like minds that worship the Almighty through their witness in love can discover new ways of interacting.

4. Cultivate A Multi-Racial/Ethnic Church

Our future is dependent on us being able to make the shift from a 93 percent Anglo-American denomination to a predominantly multi-ethnic/racial denomination. No longer can we be a majority Anglo denomination and expect to achieve significant church growth for the future. Simply put, it is demographically impossible for us to ignore this challenge and claim to be serious about growing congregations. We must be intentional about inviting persons of color into our congregations, and as partners in ministry. Our commitment to racial justice and ending racism in both our own ranks and the society is paramount to this aim. Boundary-crossing work is essential in the days ahead for both the national and local Church.

5. Train Leaders Rather Than Managers

There was a time when we valued good managers in our congregations and other governing body work. This served its purpose when financial resources were abundant. Today, we need leaders who can creatively envision a future using contextual analysis, strategic planning, and inspirational motivation to lead the Church. Too often we witness leaders who can do well when the coffers are full and pews are packed, but do not possess critical thinking skills to embrace a viable ministry direction when challenges arise.

> **Too often we witness leaders who can do well when...pews are packed, but do not possess critical thinking skills to embrace a viable ministry direction when challenges arise.**

In a time when more congregations are moving toward tent making due to funding issues and governing bodies beyond the session are feeling a financial crunch, critical thinkers – not simply managers – are needed. We must identify, train, and cultivate leaders who are capable of charting a direction that is not grounded in reckless experimentation. We have lost too many congregations and people at all levels because leadership lacked critical thinking skills.

6. Retooling Clergy and Lay Leadership to Become Contextual Ministry Leaders

As ministry changes and clergypersons need to be retooled and equipped for today's ministry realities, we are losing ground. I contend Presbyterian seminaries find themselves vacillating between expectations to be "preacher factories" for congregations and academic institutions for accrediting bodies. These pressures present tremendous challenges to meet the demands of providing relevant pastoral/prophetic leadership for the twenty-first century. This current crisis in the PC(USA) is revealing that we need a leader training institute that equips and retrains both lay and pastoral leadership at every level in the Church.

7. Develop Denominational Ministry Priorities Around Common Goals

Our framing of ministry relationships in the PC(USA) National Offices and other governing bodies throughout the denomination often tend to operate in silos. Anxiety related to denominational funding, membership loss and internal conflicts creates turf tensions leading to silos. Our work is then separated by nomenclature, structures and engagement to justify our own programmatic identities. We must discover new ways of reframing work. Partnerships should expand our work and encourage broader participation from various constituencies. Restructuring alone cannot accomplish this task. We must prayerfully think through our ecclesiology and its application in order to meet current domestic and global realities in which the Church is called to witness. Greater collaboration must be encouraged at every level of the denomination to frame partnerships across governing bodies. Overcoming fear with faith should call us to partnership for the Kingdom of God.

8. Diversify Our Training by Utilizing New Technologies

Technology must be used in appropriate ways to train, teach, inform, and engage persons with the gospel. It is important that we improve our efforts to be technologically savvy in presenting the gospel. In 2014, the PC(USA) Office of Public Witness ended a 20-year, monthly, in-office legislative information session called "Second Tuesday." The

two-hour session brought 20 to 40 Presbyterians to
Washington, DC to hear legislative briefings. And only these
20 to 40 persons were usually in attendance. The request
from this aging group for us to move the event to an online
format has now increased our reach to as many as 300
persons. We must become tech savvy at every level of the
denomination to reach both members and non-members
with the message of the gospel and other pertinent
information. We are challenged to use various media
sources (including print, television, radio, internet and other
new media) to communicate on-going and accurate
descriptions of our policies, congregational presence,
ministry opportunities and global outreach to the world.
Expanding our own media work will provide up-to-the-
minute news from around the globe regarding the
significance of the PC(USA)'s ministry and mission.

9. Movement Engagement

Congregations can no longer be isolated from the contextual
realities of young people (particularly young adults) and
expect to remain relevant. The Young Adult Volunteer
Program is expanding and growing. Our challenge is to
develop church-based ministries in local communities that
will embrace new social movements to support young adults
engaged in an activist culture. Our young people live in a
culture in which trust in government and institutions is
difficult. Their challenges to both the government and
institutions demonstrated by groups such as the Occupy
movement, Black Lives Matter and other emerging groups
must be embraced by local congregations to foster
legitimacy within established institutions and serve as buffers
against demonization directed at these young activists.
Moreover, our relevance to their cultural struggles in our
society and world must be acknowledged through
participation in the church and not relegated to a second-
class standing. Many young adults today have more

experiences, world travel and practical learning, and undergone, and overcome, more suffering than some of us have in our later adult years. We must be willing to open doors and share the church with them, including enlisting their opinions as to how to shape both the current and future church.

10. Emphasize Long Term Interim Ministries

Many of our struggling congregations are in need of long-term interim ministers whose sole role is to bring stability and generate energy. Training Congregational Revivalist Specialists may be a new category of Pastors who will study the context of a community and transition congregations for both growth and ministry development. We must not fall into the trap of selling properties that may be opportunities for new growth with some imagination. Discovering ways to maintain property by utilizing building space for nesting congregations; renting unused space to community agencies while redeveloping ministries; or calling tent-making pastors to start ministries must become the ways that we utilize properties that currently represent dying congregations. We must avoid the sale of properties in neighborhoods that provide relevance for whole communities, or may possibly become revitalized communities in the future.

11. Transforming the National Headquarters Building and General Assembly

Our national headquarters building is filled with unoccupied space and corporate renters. Parsing the strengths and weaknesses of the vast array of programs that purport to invest in pastors' and other church leaders' skills and knowledge about who we are as Presbyterians continues be a challenge in churches across the country. I can easily envision a Training Institute that would be a place of learning and retooling for pastors and other governing body leaders. This would allow us to focus on the practical tools needed to engage the church of today while providing skill development for the current trends of culturally relevant ministries. In conjunction with seminaries and other ministry leadership groups, our headquarters building could provide both space and needed technology to assist in retooling congregational leadership. The space could be utilized for community outreach and community in-reach where the community will be able to come for prayer and quiet time with the Lord, meditating on the Lord's word and engaging in transformational ministries within the Presbyterian Center. It is significant that we have a headquarters in a prominent location in the center of the city. Will we answer the call to be the church, or simply be another corporation in the center of the city? This is the question we must answer in the days ahead. I believe that there are many ways that this building and location can be utilized more effectively so that we model the power of the church to impact transformation in the global society. The challenge is to remember that we follow the ministry of Jesus and not the corporate model.

There are more considerations that we must make moving forward. I firmly believe that Presbyterians can be a significant denomination in this period of history. We must possess imagination in charting the way forward. Lack of imagination is the crux of our struggle. We must be willing to change. More importantly, we must be willing to put our faith in front of our fears. I have great hope for the PC(USA), because God through Jesus Christ is still in charge. The only question remaining is, "Do we believe?"

-JHN

Small but Fierce
Rick Ufford-Chase

As our denomination grows smaller over the next decade, it is entirely possible for our witness to the gospel to grow. My friend and colleague Emily Brewer, who is the Co-Director of the Presbyterian Peace Fellowship, recently suggested that we have the opportunity to deepen our commitment to a radical gospel as the church decreases in membership, saying, "the church I'm excited to be a part of is one that is *small but fierce*!" As far as I'm concerned that's a pretty great description of who we should be going forward.

Where once the Presbyterian Church (USA) had more than four million members and was a prominent if ponderous presence in both the social and the political scene here in the United States, we are now less than two million members and our numbers are plummeting. Some see this as a cause for alarm, but I actually believe it to be an invitation to embrace a new vision of what it means to be a church that is a much better suited to our increasingly pluralistic and secular society.

Embracing that new vision will be tricky. In the past, our emphasis has been on creating the biggest theological tent possible to welcome the greatest number of people. As we become smaller, we will need to upend our big tent orientation to become known instead for the countercultural values that will mark us as distinctive in a sea of religious opportunities. "Small," as Emily would say, "but fierce!"

For more than half a century, we in the mainline Protestant denominations have prided ourselves on our collective witness through our national organizational structures. However, it is increasingly obvious that the massive corporate structures we have constructed for governance and efficiency have become a part of the problem.

The structure of our national church is badly broken. J. Herbert Nelson is correct: this is a spiritual problem. I would add that it is also a vision problem and an organizing problem. It is not an efficiency problem, nor is it a problem related to our failure to communicate. It certainly is not the failure of one or two or ten or 300 of our national staff who do our work and all of whom are good and faithful people striving to do the most effective ministry they possibly can.

Though this entire book is about the values that I believe we must embrace as we look to the future, it is not enough to articulate a scripturally grounded vision of justice for our church. We must dismantle an institutional structure that was designed for a different era, and create a new way to organize our collective witness as Presbyterians. Our failure to take seriously the task of reimagining our fundamental institutional structures has doomed us thus far to endless attempts to rearrange the deck chairs on the Titanic: constantly reorganizing at the national level in an attempt to live within decreasing budgets, but never recognizing the ultimate futility of our efforts. Jesus' caution that we cannot put new wine in old wineskins is entirely apt, and we are foolish not to pay attention.

I myself have had a huge personal stake in the national infrastructure of our denomination in my various leadership roles, yet it is clear to me that someone needs to say out loud, "The Emperor has no clothes." Our national, corporate, unified system of being in relationship is dysfunctional, and tinkering around the edges will not solve the problem. When we ordain Presbyterians to elected office, we ask them whether they will serve with energy, creativity, imagination and love. I can think of no better articulation of what is needed at this critical moment in our history.

It is tempting to focus all of our creativity and imagination on how we will reverse the trend of our diminishing membership. This is a waste of time and a distraction from the work we are called to do. This is not because there is no way we will ever grow again, but because a focus on growth is the surest way I can think of to assure our ultimate failure. We cannot force growth through more efficient management, nor a better public relations campaign, nor a more effective funds development strategy, nor more attractive programs. Our obsession with these things makes the hollowness of our spiritual grounding more apparent with every passing day.

Growth is not a goal of the gospel.

Faithfulness is a goal of the gospel. Spreading the Good News to the places where people long for meaning is a clear goal of the gospel. Resisting Empire values of domination and power is an indisputable goal of the gospel. Growth for growth's sake is not a goal of the gospel.

In the thirty years I have been connected to the mission and ministry of the national church, the pattern resulting from our steady decline has been clear and entirely consistent. Every couple of years we've panicked as it has become obvious that our hope for growth has resulted instead in budget shortfalls. Our national staff members are told that there will be cuts, then we whittle away at the expense side of the budget. When the cutting is done, the survivors slowly lift their heads, take stock, assume a larger job description to cover for those who have gone, and carry on as faithfully as they can. Every once in a while (about every six or eight years), we create a new organizational structure, hoping the efficiencies and collaborations that we will realize through our reorganization will, this time, lead to a sense of renewal. Over those same years, we've lurched from one crisis of confidence to another among our membership, not so much because we are unable to manage our affairs but instead because we are trying to respond to a spiritual problem with managerial fixes.

We have a national church structure designed for the growing denomination of our (supposed) glory days when hundreds of program staff could be employed to do the work of the church. What we need is a structure designed for a denomination of fewer than 1.9 million members that continues to shrink quickly. That places the responsibility for our shared witness firmly among local congregations and our regional bodies whose members know we are called by God to make this work the center of our lives.

The Presbyterian Church (USA) has organized itself into a non-profit corporation that has six different agencies. Depending on the people sitting in positions of leadership, those six national agencies (which appear labyrinthine to anyone who isn't intimately connected to the work of the national church) vacillate between collegial relationships, turf protection, bemused tolerance and outright hostility. All of them are connected to one another through the parent "Presbyterian Church (USA), A Corp.," but the mechanics of the legal connections are cloudy and few people – even within the structures – seem to fully understand them.

This critique could be offered with regard to almost any large institution, but our problem is far greater because we are charged with being the church. As our resources have diminished, and as our society has grown much more polarized and litigious, managing risk has become the highest priority in most aspects of our shared ministry at the national level. My favorite line in the Presbyterian Book of Order comes from F-1.0301, which says "The Church is to be a community of faith, entrusting itself to God alone, even at the risk of losing its life." This is the moment to play to this fundamental principle that risk is at the center of the life of the church.

Further, in an effort to be fair to our employees, and to compete in the dominant culture, we have developed a salary structure that is more commensurate with corporate America than with the alternative economy Jesus appears to have had in mind. We got there for all the right reasons: a commitment to treat our employees with dignity, a desire to assure that women were paid as well as men, and the fear that we could not find the right managers to lead such a complex organization if we were unwilling to pay six-digit salaries, to name just a few. The resulting wage structure created salaries that are corporately unsustainable for the church at the high end, and personally unsustainable for our employees at the lowest. This reality is even more troubling when one recognizes that we have subcontracted out the lowest paying jobs in our corporation, and they are not even counted in our salary structures. This should sound familiar; given that it mirrors the problems many of us are trying to confront in the larger society. Perhaps the downsizing of the church is an invitation to rethink our priorities.

Above all, secrecy reigns, which is no small irony in a church that prides itself on its open and egalitarian decision-making structure. A culture of defensiveness has become the rule, and no one is encouraged to question the decisions that are made, nor their results. As trust in the national structure dissipates among lay people across the church, the natural inclination among key leaders is to circle the wagons, further exacerbating the lack of confidence and the growing stridency of those who are increasingly concerned.

I have led much smaller, but extremely complex non-profit organizations, and I understand the problem. When I have been critiqued by those whom I am leading or supervising, my first instinct has been to push back. I become defensive, or I respond that they don't understand the "big picture." The angrier and more insistent my critics become, the more I can feel the temptation to wall myself off from the naysayers. I've learned that although it is counterintuitive and hard to pull off, the far more appropriate response most often is to bring those with concerns closer in, to offer them greater access to information, and to listen carefully to the concern that they are raising. Those concerns typically point to deeper problems that I would prefer to avoid but would do well to take seriously.

The real irony is that we Presbyterians pride ourselves on our egalitarian polity and accountability that eschews the hierarchical structures of bishops for a more democratic decision-making structure in which we assume the Holy Spirit will move through our church bodies of elected members. At the national level, we strive for a non-hierarchical system of governance in which lay people from across the denomination provide support for the work of our hired staff. However, the elected members of our governing committees who are tasked with providing both direction and oversight to the corporation discover a culture that doesn't encourage hard questions. They are carefully managed in the name of efficiency, and when they do raise significant questions, voice their reservations, or attempt to lift up new possibilities, their voices seem to be swallowed up into a quagmire of opaque committee process.

This seems like the appropriate moment to remind the reader of the excellent advice I received from my mentor, John Fife: Evil isn't primarily about bad people, it is what happens when good people get caught up in institutions that have lost the capacity to do the right thing. There is not a person I can think of within this system who isn't trying to do their level best. I've seen a series of leadership changes at the highest levels for nearly three decades, but the structural problems persist.

Here I want to return to the 25th Chapter of the Gospel of Matthew. Remember that the chapter is made up of three stories. The first is the story of the bridesmaids in waiting, and the clear instruction to ready ourselves for what is coming next. The second is the story of the third slave who chose to resist the hard taskmaster and refused to participate in a system of economic oppression that would take unfair advantage of his neighbors. The third is the story of the Judgment of the Nations.

Having been clear in his critique of the dominant economic paradigm, Jesus shares a parable that clarifies what will be most highly valued in the community he envisions. When the Day of Judgment comes, he says, we will be separated into those who find favor with God and those who do not. The things that society seems to value – wealth and power in particular – will have no bearing whatsoever on who is judged to be worthy. Instead, the question will be whether we cared for those most in need: the hungry, the thirsty, the stranger, the destitute, the sick, and the imprisoned. Further, this judgment will be applied not just to individuals, but to nations. We will be held to this standard corporately.

> When the Son of Man comes in his glory, and all the angels with him, then he will sit on the throne of his glory. All the nations will be gathered before him, and he will separate people one from another as a shepherd separates the sheep from the goats, and he will put the sheep at his right hand and the goats at the left. Then the king will say to those at his right hand, 'Come, you that are blessed by my Father, inherit the kingdom prepared for you from the foundation of the world; for I was hungry and you gave me food, I was thirsty and you gave me something to drink, I was a stranger and you welcomed me, I was naked and you gave me clothing, I was sick and you took care of me, I was in prison and you visited me.' Then the righteous will answer him, 'Lord, when was it that we saw you hungry and gave you food, or thirsty and gave you something to drink? And when was it that we saw you a stranger and welcomed you, or naked and gave you clothing? And when was it that we saw you sick or in prison and visited you?' And the king will answer them, 'Truly I tell you, just as you did it to one of the least of these who are members of my family, you did it to me.' Then he will say to those at his left hand, 'You that are accursed, depart from me into the eternal fire prepared for the devil and his angels; for I was hungry and you gave me no food, I was thirsty and you gave me nothing to drink, I was a stranger and you did not welcome me, naked and you did not give me clothing, sick and in prison and you did not

visit me.' Then they also will answer, 'Lord, when was it that we saw you hungry or thirsty or a stranger or naked or sick or in prison, and did not take care of you?' Then he will answer them, 'Truly I tell you, just as you did not do it to one of the least of these, you did not do it to me.' And these will go away into eternal punishment, but the righteous into eternal life. (Matthew 25:31-46)

This passage has been the most influential in my life. When I took that year-long class in discipleship as a junior in high school, this story captivated me. It has given me purpose for thirty-five years, changing and deepening as new experiences have opened me to a more profound reading of the parable.

What would it look like if we put Matthew 25 at the heart of every move we make as we reimagine our national church structure? I recently heard Jim Wallis, co-founder of the Sojourners community, offer the suggestion that placing ourselves in proximity to the places where people are suffering or experiencing oppression is as much a spiritual discipline as prayer is. What if this were the fundamental question driving our collective witness as a church?

> What would it look like if we put Matthew 25 at the heart of every move we make as we reimagine our national church structure?

Here's what I think that might look like:

1. We will call leaders primarily for their vision, integrity, and understanding of the gospel imperative – not for managerial expertise, which will become far less important as we dramatically downsize the infrastructure of the church.

2. We will pay salaries that are enough to live on comfortably and no more, with the assumption that the leaders we seek will be prepared to serve at those salaries because they understand it to be an act of faithfulness. God will provide the leaders we need. Of that, I am certain.

3. Though I appreciate J. Herbert's idea of rethinking the use of our national offices in Kentucky, my own thinking has gone in a different direction. In my estimation, we will likely have to give up the national church offices and move our national staff into the at-risk communities around the country where we already have appropriate infrastructure: churches in the inner city or rural communities, camp and conference centers that are fully engaged in shaping the next generation to save their own watersheds, intentional communities where we choose to live as an expression of our commitment to stand against the dominant culture, places where disasters have struck.

4. We'll use technology to connect us to one another to share ideas and collaborate. We'll forego offices and cubicles for real engagement in house churches and justice projects that are getting to the heart of what it means to be church in the heart of an inhospitable Empire. Using current and developing technology and tools as they are available, we'll connect and collaborate.

5. Though there will always be a need for a small cadre of people who are compensated in order to help coordinate our work, there will be far less distinction between staff and volunteers. Instead, we will focus on developing teams of people – volunteers and paid staff together – who are passionate about their call to do the work of shaping our collective witness as the people of God.

6. We will continue a transition we've already begun from a culture of institutional protection to a permission-giving culture

that is daring, risky, creative and bold. The trick will be to seek leaders who know how to maintain just enough institutional stability to sustain our witness while assuring that there is plenty of room for the Spirit to move.

7. The function of our national staff will be primarily to coordinate the gatherings of those who are passionate about mission, or theology, or solidarity, or the witness of our faith.

8. The standard against which we will evaluate our work will be whether we are effectively empowering and encouraging the whole church to put the 25th Chapter of Matthew at the center of our lives together.

So how do we get there? I propose we begin with a listening project, in which we reach out to two groups: our elders who offer the fundamental values that have carried us through similarly challenging times, and others who currently would not be caught dead (there's an interesting turn of phrase) in a traditional church but who are taking on the big challenges I've laid out in this book, and who are open and curious about their spirituality. Pastor Mike McGrath, a fourth-generation Pentecostal from California and a leader in the Black Lives Matter movement, recently told the crowd at the Festival of Faiths that our young people are far more interested in courage than they are in church. Think about that for a minute...

We should spend a focused period of time listening to these two key groups – the elders among us who have a history of taking risks, and people who are modeling the daring love of Jesus but don't show up in church – and reflect what we are hearing back to the broader church. In the Presbyterian Church we have a unique office of Moderator of the General Assembly that lends itself to this function. We must listen well, then articulate a vision that will excite both those inside and outside of the church. This is not about surveys and opinion polls that our leaders then regurgitate in an effort to gain popularity. Any politician can do that, and it is entirely unimpressive and equally unimaginative.

We need leaders who can craft a compelling vision. That demands both the skill of active listening and the courage to lead the church where it does not yet know that it needs to go. This will not be easy, especially since we are beginning with a serious breach of trust about our intentions that exists both inside and outside the walls of our churches.

However, our commitment to the gospel offers a significant benefit. Time and again, I have seen sisters and brothers in the faith subvert their own desires and even their self-interest in order to help the church be more faithful. We must trust our national and regional staff, our clergy and the people in our pews, and even those who have left the pews, to do the right thing. This demands a significant shift in our culture. Currently we don't trust our staff to put aside their own interests, we don't trust our lay people to have the expertise, the passion or the commitment to actually take responsibility for leading the church, and we don't even know the people who aren't showing up on Sunday morning.

So let's make our national and regional staff our allies in the work of transforming the church instead of treating them as the objects of our decision making. Let's assume that God has chosen those on the national committees of the church to lead us with conviction during these troubled times. Let's engage all of our key stakeholders, especially national staff and committee members and our partners in our regional governing bodies, in a process of imagining the church of twenty years from now. Then, let's be proactive and bold. Let's agree to actually become that church in five years.

Our national staff should be invited, rather than compelled, to help us imagine and implement an entirely new way of being church. We should explain that at the end of five years they are quite likely to have worked themselves out of a job, that they are welcome to leave if they feel called away, and that we trust them to give us their best effort in imagining this new thing we are being called to create. Committee members should be asked to step back if they don't feel that the all-absorbing work of transforming our national church is something that they are called to give their heart and soul to, and we should call new leaders forward based on their passion and vision for creating an entirely new way of being the national church in this challenging but exciting time!

I am extremely hopeful about the future for all kinds of reasons. The spirit is on the move in the Presbyterian Church (USA) and beyond, and there is a pretty decent chance that we can remake ourselves into something new and different just as we have in the past. That's what Martin Luther and John Calvin taught us. It's what we learn when we read through our Book of Confessions and recognize all the ways in which the church has grappled with change in the past. It's what happens when leaders like J. Herbert Nelson step forward to offer a vision for the future of the church – a development that took place after I invited J. Herbert to write for this chapter.

This is our moment! We have the chance to participate in a broad movement of the Holy Spirit. That Spirit cannot be contained by institutional boundaries or a corporate structure designed primarily for managerial efficiency in bygone days. Something new is in the wind. God is calling us to claim our heritage of "reformed and always being reformed," and to live insisting that we will no longer be the church of Empire, but instead will follow Jesus to the edge of the Empire.

Small – but fierce!

Discussion Questions:

1. Reread the story of the Judgment of the Nations in Matthew 25. What has this passage meant to you in the past? How does it speak to you now?

2. J. Herbert has offered a list of eleven things he would like to propose for rethinking our national witness. Given his recent nomination to become the Stated Clerk of the Presbyterian Church (USA), those ideas have particular currency. Which ones do you resonate with?

3. Think of a time you have been involved in implementing a significant organizational change. What were the challenges? What worked and what didn't?

4. Rick has shared some of his ideas about how the national church might look different for the church of the future. What are your ideas? What do you think of his?

Conclusion
Everything in this story is true...

Bicycle Quilt Village
Michael Benefiel

Everything in this story is true, except the part that hasn't happened yet...

Once upon a time, a miracle arrived in a dusty hill village in the southwestern mountains. Up from the broad flat fields of the plains came a grandfather named Jose and a grandmother named Maria. Both rode on bicycles and carried backpacks full of wonders.

From inside Maria's backpack came steel needles and colored threads and scraps of cloth from many different places. She taught the grandmothers of the village, which had a different name then, how to sew new designs in quilts with these new colors – the yellow of the desert, the blue of the river, the red of the sunset, the rainbow colors of sky and sea and earth. Once the grandmothers learned how to quilt, they taught the mothers, and then the mothers taught their daughters. And word of the quilts began to spread from village to village.

From inside Jose's backpack came steel tools and metal parts and small pots of bright paints. He taught the grandfathers how to make bicycles with gears that changed and shiny metal parts, chains with strong links, pedals, wheels with spokes, baskets and lights and bells. Grandfathers taught fathers and fathers taught the sons of the village. Word of the bicycles began to spread. Now visitors began to come and ask directions to "Bicycle Quilt Village."

From time to time, there were boys who learned to quilt and girls who learned to make bicycles. The villagers smiled and agreed that children should follow their talents and have a chance to show what they could do. Work rewarded the thought and efforts of each person. Quilts and bicycles connected them with each other. The villagers found pride in the making of useful and beautiful things, and they were delighted with the miracles. Sometimes they would ride their bicycles to the towns of the plains to buy more metal pieces and paints for new bicycles and colors for threads and cloth for quilts.

One day a tempting offer came from the men of the city. The city men proposed to trade quilts and bicycles from the village for new machines that could sew faster. At first, most of the women said they liked the old ways. The work of sewing allowed for gathering and talking, listening to one another and sharing joys and sorrows, sometimes singing in harmony. "What good would more quilts bring to the village?" the women asked. "Don't we already have what we need to keep ourselves warm and trade with our neighbors?"

The loudest men did not share the wishes of their daughters and wives and mothers. They said that the women could find another time to talk with each other. Some quieter men worried that the new machines would be noisy and ugly and thought the women might be right. The temptations of more wealth and power dazzled some of the men (and even a few of the women). Many thought that the new machines would do their work for them, so they could relax and go fishing. They would no longer have to make an effort to work together and could leave the hard work to others.

The Bicycle Quilt Village enjoyed their new machines at first. The machines were, as feared, noisy and ugly and smelly. Still, the work changed and more quilts were made. One quilt began to look like another, because it was simpler to pick one or two designs and make them over and over. Women didn't find the work enjoyable because the singing, talking, and sharing stopped. Soon, the women of Bicycle Quilt Village began to forget who they were. The machines were a dark presence in the center of the village. The joys of shared creation and caring conversations as hands and hearts produced beautiful and loving work – all that goodness began to disappear into the dark.

The machines brought more than darkness and separation to the Bicycle Quilt Village and its families. Soon, city men began to organize competitions for bicycles and quilts. Outsiders came to bring their expert words to the villages: big words like "economic productivity" and "technological innovation" and "efficient deployment of the factors of production." No expert words like "soul" or "spirit" or "community" or "interdependent network of mutuality" were heard in the village. Jose and Maria, who might have spoken those words, quietly left this village and moved away, with tears in their eyes and sadness in their hearts.

Changes that came to quilts also came to bicycles. The people of Bicycle Quilt Village learned how to borrow money from city people. They began, one by one, to make ends meet by serving the machines and taking small advantage of weaker neighbors. They borrowed more and they never seemed able to repay what they owed.

A double crisis came. A fire burned the quilting place. After heavy rains, a flood came to destroy the bicycle factory, rusting the metal parts and burying the tools in thick mud. All work stopped, though the lenders wanted to be paid anyway.

The families of Bicycle Quilt Village gathered in the field and cried out in their loss and misfortune and confusion. They even called upon the king and the city people and the big word experts. No one came to help, except a big word expert who earned money by advising about disasters. The families of

Bicycle Quilt Village looked for Jose and Maria to ask for more miracles. They were nowhere to be found. They had gone to another place.

The loud people found words to blame others for all the misfortunes of Bicycle Quilt Village. They pointed their fingers and found fault and vented anger. One by one, the loud people shouted and complained.

Patiently, the quieter people listened, remembering that the loud people had said other things and promised happiness before the machines and the darkness had come. The quiet people looked at one another, waiting for the loud people to finish. The disaster expert told the villagers that they were hopeless, unable to manage their own recovery, and needed to borrow more money from the city people. The quiet people thought many thoughts, for they were also angry – at themselves for allowing loud people to bully them. After many days, each person had listened and spoken and a silence came to Bicycle Quilt Village.

Out of this silence, a young woman stood up. Her name was Marguerite and she was the oldest daughter in her family, often busy helping her mother with the younger children. Marguerite said, "I have an idea for a new quilt design and I have some leftover threads. By myself, I don't have enough material to make a quilt. Will anyone join me to make a new quilt together?"

Before the villagers could answer, the disaster expert laughed in a mean way and gave a dozen reasons why this idea would never work. All were silent.

"I remember the old times when our work had meaning and we shared our lives with one another," said a young man named Miguelito. "I am not so good at quilting, Marguerite, but I do have some metal parts and I remember how to make a good bicycle. Will anyone join me to make a new bicycle together?"

The Bicycle Quilt Village people looked at the burned place and the flooded place. They looked at each other. Then the people who wanted to make quilts began to stand with Marguerite, and the people who wanted to build bicycles moved to stand with Miguelito. They waved their hands and bid a polite farewell to the disaster expert, who shook his head and left, bitter that the village would not pay him for advice. Instead of believing the disaster expert, the people trusted their own memories of the past and dreams for a different future. Day by day, they found their way back to a community rich in happiness and health, if not always up to date with the dazzling distractions of the city.

Now if you want to go and visit Bicycle Quilt Village, you have to drive your car to the end of the road and park. You'll find a bicycle waiting for you. You are welcome to bicycle into the streets of Bicycle Quilt Village. The community is restored because the people followed the youthful hopes of Marguerite and Miguelito. They found a way to care for one another and to do the good work of making beautiful things together.

Once a year, at the fire and flood festival, they sing songs to remember Jose and Maria. They ask a clown to dress as the disaster expert and everyone laughs together as his big words bounce around the audience. They sing songs for children, who will become leaders soon, and need to discover for themselves what work and community can mean.

When neighbors ask Bicycle Quilt Village for help, partners go over to accompany them. They ride their bicycles and carry knapsacks full of miracles. They share ancient wisdom and open hearts and the promise that we can heal ourselves and our interdependent and broken world.

-MB

Our Jubilee Moment
Rick Ufford-Chase

Ross and Gloria Kinsler trained at the ecumenical Missionary Orientation Center at Stony Point Center in the early 1960's, and then left for a career in Central America. In 1999, Orbis Books published a remarkable book that they co-wrote called *The Biblical Jubilee and the Struggle for Life*. The book had a huge impact on me when it was first published, and it was one of many that I reviewed during this writing project. Their thesis is that Jesus intentionally adopted the radical themes of economic liberation from the Jubilee texts in Hebrew scripture, and that his ministry was all about calling for a new jubilee, an economic liberation, for the poor and oppressed of his time.

To share just one, specific example, their reading of the Lord's Prayer totally upended my understanding of the most fundamental practice of my life as a Christian. The words I had been reciting almost my entire life took on a far more revolutionary meaning as I read them with new eyes:

> Our Father in heaven,
>   Hallowed be your name.
> Your kingdom come.
> Your will be done,
>   On earth as it is in heaven.
> Give us this day our daily bread.
> And forgive us our debts,
>   As we also have forgiven our debtors.
> And do not bring us to the time of trial,
>   But rescue us from the evil one.
>   (Matthew 6:9-13)

"What does the coming of God's reign mean? It means, first, to ask that God's will be done here on Earth and not just in heaven, as revealed in the Law and the Prophets. It means,

second, to ask for 'our daily bread,' no more and no less, which is, as we learned from Exodus 16, a Sabbath Day mandate. It means, third, to be forgiven of debts and to forgive debts, which is, as we say in Deuteronomy 15, a Sabbath Year mandate. Finally, it means to resist the evil one, who tempts God's people, as he tempted Jesus, to disobey and break the covenant with Yahweh. The Lord's Prayer is a call to Sabbath – Jubilee spirituality as envisioned for the tribes of Yahweh in the Promised Land, a socioeconomic possibility that Israel abandoned under the monarchy so that some could become rich and powerful and others would become poor and marginalized."[1]

I had recited that prayer at least once a week every year of my life. By the time I read the Kinslers' book I was in my mid-thirties and had been reconsidering many scripture passages in light of more than ten years of experience on the U.S./Mexico border. Still, I had never paused to consider the words I was repeating in the Lord's Prayer. Nearly twenty years later, my understanding has shifted once again as I have realized that this text is liberationist not just for those who have been actively marginalized and excluded from the Empire, but also for those of us who have forgotten, like the people of the Bicycle Quilt Village, our fundamental values.

What would it look like to claim this as a jubilee moment in the life of our church? What if we accounted for the ways in which we have embraced the wrong vision, corrected for our own excess, and returned to the heart of what it means to be the people of God? What if we chose this moment to let go of the church we have labored so much to build in order to become active participants – co-creators – with God, in this act of imagination to renew our

---

[1] Gloria Kinsler and Ross Kinsler, *The Biblical Jubilee and the Struggle for Life: An Invitation to Personal, Ecclesial, and Social Transformation* (Ossining, NY: Orbis Books, 1999), 100-101.

witness as followers of Jesus, the risen Lord and the Prince of Peace?

Our sacred text is replete with stories of God's people being held to account at similarly challenging moments in history. The proposals put forward in this book may not be the only way to be faithful, nor is this the only way to read scripture, but I believe that it is an ethic that is deeply ingrained in our tradition as Christians. If our churches model what has been described in this book and commit to re-form our Christian community to take seriously the great challenges we confront - we will have something unique and important to offer the broader community.

If people in the United States want a fundamentalist approach to the bible, there are plenty of churches where they can find it. If they are looking for an evangelical approach in which evangelicalism is practiced as political and social conservatism and the bible is interpreted through the lens of personal piety, they will have no trouble finding churches that embody that theology and offer a community in which they will feel right at home. If there are those who seek a church that justifies the excesses of Empire, those churches are ubiquitous and they should choose one. But what is largely missing from the religiously pluralistic landscape in the United States in this historical moment is an authentic, inclusive, biblically-grounded church that is willing to recognize its own complicity in systemic structures of injustice and stand, without apology, for a just and sustainable future.

Right now, we could reclaim our prophetic voice and make it clear that we cannot bless the forces of social and economic colonization. Right now, we could call out those who refuse to take responsibility for climate change, and offer a new ethic for fully inhabiting our watersheds and righting the damage we have done to creation. Right now, we could reject religious exceptionalism and insist that we will allow neither subtle nor overt attempts to use Christianity as a justification for violence and military aggression. Though there

210 \ Faithful Resistance

are different ways to interpret scripture, it would be difficult to assert that such a prophetic witness is not deeply ingrained in our sacred text and our historical tradition.

We should engage our greatest challenges head-on. In a time of fearfulness, the temptation toward caution and a return to the familiar is deceptively seductive. Instead, this is another direction we could choose to go. Like the people of Bicycle Quilt Village, we could uncover the faint memories of what called us into being and begin again: a few brightly colored strands at a time, a few parts and a simple bicycle at a time.

Remember, this is a "what if" book. The authors whom I asked to collaborate are backed by dozens, maybe even hundreds of others who are already practicing new ways of forming local Christian communities and regional associations that have remembered who they are. What if we could inspire many more such efforts, and what if we backed those efforts with a bold and unapologetic commitment to justice and earth care? In my own Presbyterian tradition, we have made tentative, but thoughtful and conscious, choices to embrace these challenges as a part of our collective witness to the power of the gospel.

We have affirmed gay marriage. We've discerned together that we are called to stand against war and embrace nonviolence as our first response to situations of both structural oppression and overt acts of violence. We have offered a strong critique of the gun industry and the epidemic of gun violence in our country. We have wrestled with serious questions about how to be faithful partners for peace in the Middle East, and affirmed that we will screen our investments in an effort to withdraw our support from companies that are complicit in Israel's occupation of Palestine, as well as those that support extremists who use terror as a weapon in Israel or anywhere in the world. We have affirmed an "Interreligious Stance" that makes it clear we are choosing to be partners with those of other religious traditions in our increasingly pluralistic society. At our General Assembly in 2016, we will consider whether to divest our financial investments from companies whose core enterprise is fossil fuel extraction. Slowly, but surely, we have been laying the groundwork to reclaim the basis for an anti-Empire ethic.

I know that the cost has been high, but I believe that act of faithfulness will help us to thrive in our pluralistic landscape. Becoming just like everyone else is a recipe for meaninglessness and irrelevance. Christians, if we are to have any currency in the multi-religious landscape of the United States, must be clear that we will not back down from the gospel values of the 25th Chapter of Matthew. Like the five bridesmaids who tended their lamps, we are ready to step into the unknown. Like the third slave who refused to take advantage of his sisters and brothers for his own or his master's gain, we withdraw our consent from the dominant culture. Like the sheep gathered at the right hand of the Son of Man, we stand with the poor, the dispossessed, the sick, the foreigner, and the incarcerated.

We will count the real cost of what it means to be Christian.

As I reread the Kinslers' book, I found a prayer that I had forgotten, but that had a significant impact on me when I first read it. It is a "Prayer for a "People in the Throes of Martyrdom" written by Fernando Bermúdez during the unspeakable violence of the war in Guatemala in the 1980's, which is where I began my own conversion to the Christian faith after having been raised in a Christian church all my life.

> Lord, may your Gospel be for me not a book,
> But Good News, lived and shared.
> May I not be embittered by oppression
> May I speak more of hope than of calamities.
> May my denunciations be first subjected to discernment,
> in community,
> brought before you in profound prayer,

and uttered without arrogance,
not as an instrument of aggression,
but neither with timidity and cowardice.
May I never resign myself to the exploitation of the poor,
In whatever form it may come.
Help me to be subversive of any unjust order.
Help me to be free,
And to struggle for the freedom of the oppressed.
May I never become accustomed to the suffering of the martyrs
 and the news that my brothers and sisters are enduring
  Persecution,
but may their lives and witness ever move me to conversion
and to the greatest loyalty to the Kingdom.
May I accept my church with an ever growing love
and with Christian realism.
May I not reject it for its faults,
 but feel myself committed to renew it,
 and help it to be what you, Lord, want it to be.
May I fear not death, but infidelity.[2]

My friends, this is our moment. If we choose to let it go by, we will never overcome our regret. Let's take a risk.

-RUC

---

[2] Fernando Bermúdez, *Death and Resurrection in Guatemala* (Ossining, NY: Orbis Books, 1986), 74-75

Discussion Questions:

1. Michael Benefiel wrote the Bicycle Quilt Village in a workshop at Ghost Ranch led by Rick in 2007. In an exercise borrowed from John Paul Lederach, Rick asked the participants to write an imaginative essay that began with the statement "Everything in this story is true, except for the part that hasn't happened yet..." Having read Rick's book, what would your own essay say?

2. What do you believe about Rick's assertion that we must claim a distinctive witness of what it means to be Christian if we are to have any relevance in our religiously pluralistic society today?

3. Rick has framed this as a jubilee moment. What does that mean to you? Are there other jubilee texts that you have found to be particularly meaningful?

4. In Guatemala in the 1980's, hundreds of thousands of Christians were targeted, along with many others in the civil society, for their work defending basic dignity and human rights. Two hundred thousand people were murdered or "disappeared" and hundreds more Guatemalan villages were wiped out by the repressive Guatemalan government and military, backed by the United States. Given that context, what do you think about Rick's choice to end his book with the prayer written by Fernando Bermúdez? How is resisting Empire in the United States similar today, and how is it different?

Acknowledgments

This book is a testament to the fact that I myself have been a community project. There are too many people to thank, for the ideas that I shared in this book have been shaped and formed by hundreds of people. However, it is clear that they would have remained ideas in my head and never been published if it weren't for my friends and editors at UnShelved. I'm deeply grateful to Aric Clark, my dialogue partner in this project, to Carol Howard Merritt for her willingness to mentor me and to reform my writing, and to Megan Dosher Hansen for her thoughtful attention to maintaining each contributor's voice. UnShelved is, all by itself, a classic example of the church of the future. May there be many projects to come.

And . . . Thanks to the Community of Living Traditions in which I live. You teach me how to be more faithful with each passing day.

Contributors

Annanda Barclay

Annanda Barclay is a candidate for ordination in the PC(USA). She is a graduate of Austin Presbyterian Theological Seminary, and a Fund for Theological Education Ministry Fellow. She co-moderates the More Light Presbyterians, and blogs for Believe Out Loud. She is an advocate for intersectional justice, love and kindness. Annanda is the Pastoral Intern at First Presbyterian Church in Palo Alto, California. Annanda has a deep reverence for God's grace made manifest in how we love and honor ourselves and God's creations. She enjoys pilgrimaging about life, nerding out on eco-housing, and finding the Divine in the outdoors, strangers, friends, family, and her beloved dog Wes.

Michael Benefiel

Michael Benefiel is a Unitarian Universalist whose first career was as a U.S. Diplomat. He spent nine years in Japan, first as a student, and later as a part of his diplomatic service. After retirement, Michael took a 40-hour mediation training in 2008. Since then, he has worked with Day-of-Trial programs in District Court and volunteered with the Conflict Resolution Center of Montgomery County, Maryland. Michael was instrumental in the planning for the Christian Peace Witness for Iraq in March, 2007, which filled the National Cathedral in Washington, D.C., and led to

224 arrests for nonviolent civil disobedience in front of the White House.

Aric Clark

The Rev. Aric Clark is a writer, speaker, and Presbyterian minister who lives in Portland, Oregon, with his wife and two gremlins pretending to be his sons. He is the co-author of *Never Pray Again: Lift Your Head, Unfold Your Hands, and Get To Work*, a book which challenges readers to embrace a concrete other-centered spirituality. He is also the creator of *LectionARIC*, a YouTube channel for hermeneutical vlogs. When he is not writing, preaching, or parenting, Aric can be found engaging his tabletop gaming hobby, or cooking for a crowd of random strangers he invited home without his wife's permission. He is a pacifist, and he still can't grow a beard.

Linda Eastwood

The Rev. Dr. Linda Eastwood is a PC(USA) Teaching Elder, ordained as coordinator of the Colombia Accompaniment Program. After 25 years as a physicist designing MRI systems, Linda earned her MDiv at McCormick Theological Seminary. She now is an affiliate faculty member at McCormick Theological Seminary, specializing in the dialogue between Religion and Science. She has taught at the Lutheran School of Theology in Chicago and the Reformed University in Barranquilla, Colombia. She serves on the board of the

Chicago Religious Leadership Network on Latin America, and on the PC(USA) Advisory Committee on Social Witness Policy.

Alison Harrington

The Reverend Alison J. Harrington is the pastor of Southside Presbyterian Church in Tucson, Arizona. She earned a bachelor's degree in Peace and Conflict Studies with an emphasis in U.S. Race Relations from UC Berkeley, and a Master of Divinity from San Francisco Theological Seminary (SFTS). In 2011 she was awarded the Beatitudes Society Brave Preacher Award and was a Beatitudes Society Fellow in 2013-2014. In the Fall of 2014, Alison was named by the Center for American Progress as one of 15 Faith Leaders to Watch in 2015. Most recently she was named the 2016 Distinguished Alumna by SFTS.

Rabia Terri Harris

Rabia Terri Harris is Chaplain and Scholar in Residence at the Community of Living Traditions at Stony Point Center. Rabia founded the Muslim Peace Fellowship as an associate organization of the Fellowship of Reconciliation in 1994. Rabia received her religious education through the Halveti-Jerrahi Order. She holds degrees from Princeton University, Columbia University and Hartford Seminary. In 2009, Rabia served as the first president of the Association of Muslim Chaplains. Her contributions to this chapter are excerpted from a lecture offered at the 2015

Lake Junaluska Peace Conference; you can access the full paper at academia.edu.

Pastor Jin S. Kim

Jin is founding pastor of Church of All Nations in Minneapolis, Minnesota, and chief cultural architect of Underground Seminary. He grew up in the deep South after emigrating from Korea with his family at age 7. He went to Georgia Tech, Princeton Seminary, has a DMin from Columbia Seminary, and has served as a congregational pastor since 1993. Exasperated by the arduous task of deprogramming seminary grads in CAN's internship program, Jin thought it'd be better to equip them to be radical disciples from the start. Jin's household includes his wife Soon Pac and teenagers Claire & Austin.

Alex Patchin McNeill

Alex Patchin McNeill is the first openly transgender person to head a mainline Protestant organization. He is an openly transgender man, a life-long Presbyterian, and a nationally known educator and advocate for lesbian, gay, bisexual, transgender and queer (LGBTQ) Christians. He played key roles in organizing faith communities for the passage of Amendment 10A in the PC(USA), and for marriage equality legislation in Maryland. His journey to ordination is currently being chronicled in the documentary, Out of Order. Alex holds a Master of Divinity from Harvard Divinity School, and a bachelor's degree from the University of North Carolina – Chapel Hill.

Brian Merritt

Brian Merritt is the organizing Evangelist of Mercy Junction Justice and Peace Center in Chattanooga, Tennessee and the preacher at Renaissance Presbyterian Church. Brian is the founding member of Unconference at Stony Point Center and San Francisco Theological Seminary. Brian served as the Senior Pastor of the ecumenical church The Palisades Community Church and helped found the Social Justice Circle of the Interfaith Conference of Metropolitan Washington. While in Washington, Brian was instrumental in pushing for marriage equality in the district and advocated for marriage equality in the Presbyterian Church (USA). He also organized the protest chaplains of Occupy DC and 9/11 Unity Walk.

Ched Myers

Ched Myers is an activist theologian who has worked in social change movements for 40 years. He is a popular educator who animates scripture and issues of faith-based peace and justice (his many articles and half-dozen books can be found at www.ChedMyers.org). A Mennonite, Ched has worked with a variety of social justice organizations, including the American Friends Service Committee.

He is a co-founder of several collaborative projects, including the Center and Library for the Bible and Social Justice (http://clbsj.org/) and the Watershed Discipleship Alliance (http://watersheddiscipleship.org/). He and his partner Elaine Enns, a restorative justice practitioner, live in southern California and co-direct Bartimaeus Cooperative Ministries (www.bcm-net.org).

J. Herbert Nelson, II

The Reverend Dr. J. Herbert Nelson, II, Director of the Presbyterian Church (USA) Office of Public Witness (OPW) in Washington, D.C., is a third generation Presbyterian pastor. Before coming to Washington, he served as founder/pastor of Liberation Community Presbyterian Church in Memphis, Tennessee. Nelson has degrees from Johnson C. Smith University, Johnson C. Smith Seminary at the Interdenominational Theological Center, and Louisville Presbyterian Theological Seminary. J. Herbert was recently nominated for the position of Stated Clerk of the Presbyterian Church (USA). Nelson is married to the Reverend Gail Porter Nelson and together they are parents of an adult daughter.

John Nelson

John grew up on a farm near Blue Earth, Minnesota. After graduating from Bethel University and Bethel Seminary, he served as coordinator of the Internship Program at Church of All Nations (CAN) from 2009-2013, focusing on pastoral training of seminary graduates through intensive "life together." This experience informs his recently completed MTh thesis at Luther Seminary, where Bonhoeffer's ecclesiology and Bourdieu's social theory has helped him rethink ministry in our age of neoliberal globalization. John currently serves as Parish Instructor at CAN, and lives at the Fink House with his wife, Seulgee, and the seminary students.

Laura Newby

Laura was born and raised in rural Wisconsin before moving to Minneapolis-St. Paul to attend college. After a year teaching English in South Korea, she returned to Minnesota in 2006 where she found and fell in love with Church of All Nations (CAN). Deeply transformed by the church's critical analysis of western ideology on the one hand, and its hospitable and intimate community on the other, she committed herself to the lifelong work of decolonizing herself and the church. She is a co-founder of Underground Seminary and serves as Ministry Assistant at Church of All Nations.

Germán Zárate

Germán Zárate Durier: Germán is a ruling elder and co-ordinator of the National Office of "Diaconía" (Social Service and Justice) of the Presbyterian Church of Colombia (IPC). One of his roles is to ensure that each IPC Presbytery is prepared to receive the accompaniers they request, sent through the Presbyterian Peace Fellowship (PPF). Germán has studied theology (Mexico and Costa Rica), Sociology (Costa Rica), and social pedagogy (Cartagena, Colombia). Germán also teaches in the Reformed University in Barranquilla and "extension" courses in Urabá. Germán lives in Barranquilla with his wife Teresita Bustamente, their daughter, Laura Isabel, and their son, Alejandro.

Cover Artist

Mary Button
Born and raised in East Texas, Mary Button received a BFA in Photography and Imaging at the Tisch School of the Arts at New York University. She earned a Master's of Theological Studies with a concentration in American religious history and Christian ethics from the Candler School of Theology at Emory University. Her work has  been exhibited across the United States and the United Kingdom. She currently serves First Congregational Church in Memphis, TN as their Minister of Art. When she's not creating work in her studio, she's teaching art in women's prisons.

Author: Rick Ufford-Chase

Rick Ufford-Chase was the Moderator of the 216th General Assembly of the Presbyterian Church (USA), from 2004 to 2006. He is a lifelong activist and advocate for social justice. He served in various capacities in mission on the U.S./Mexico border for nearly twenty years, where he was a co-founder of BorderLinks, Samaritans and No More Deaths. In 2008, Rick and his wife Kitty became the Co-Directors of Stony Point Center, where they helped to found the Community of Living Traditions, a multifatih, residential community of Muslims, Christians and Jews who dedicate themselves to the practice of hospitality, nonviolence, peace and justice. He currently also serves part-time as the Associate Director for Interfaith Formation for the Presbyterian Mission Agency. Rick is the Co-Moderator of the Activist Council for the Presbyterian Peace Fellowship. Rick is the father of three, Leana (17), Troy (18) and Teo (21). He is an avid outdoorsman whose first loves are rafting, kayaking, and sailing.

46627902R00126

Made in the USA
San Bernardino, CA
15 March 2017